SASHA VLAD

SLIDING RUINS

DAN STANCIU

< Other Collaborations >

Dan Stanciu & Sasha Vlad
Parazitul azurului/Le parasite de l'azur/
The parasite of the azure,
Local Tare, Bucharest, 2006

Dan Stanciu & Sasha Vlad
Borbro, Feen, Serliq, Obs, Kabupaten,
Duamaa, Epona, Snijngad, Ek-Yolo, Sodhi,
Jumah, Burcep, Lecade,
Locul Tare, Bucharest, 2005

Gheorghe Rasovszky, Dan Stanciu,
Julian Tanase, Sasha Vlad
Before/After; 52 Trans-visual Apparitions
Generated by Chance
Editura ICARE, Bucharest, 2003

SLIDING

65 Drawings/

Commentary

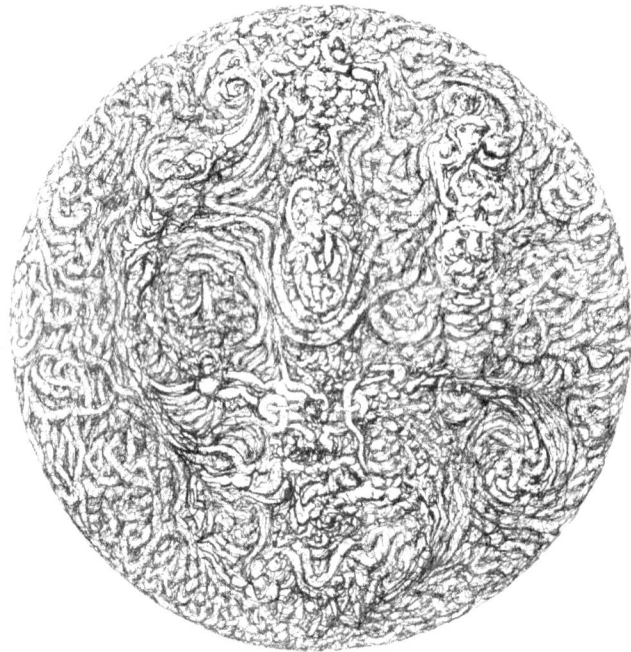

RUINS

Sasha Vlad

65 Poems/ Dan Stanciu

Bruno Solarik

Rêve à Deux

Bucharest - San Francisco – Vacaville

ISBN 978-0-578-19132-4

SLIDING RUINS

1

Risk and drift are contact weapons, which cannot strike, but can liberate. (For foxes, during the stone-still period, one can use cautiously the chromatic scalpel. For the knotted animals, such as the vagrant armoire, for fruits from the fountain family, or for the mechanical apparitions, in which hides the sock-panther when it has cubs, we would recommend the consuming embrace from the East backwards.)

As vital weapons, the risk and drift diminish the combatants' orientation capacity on the screen of a day, but they increase their ability of sculpting the battle.

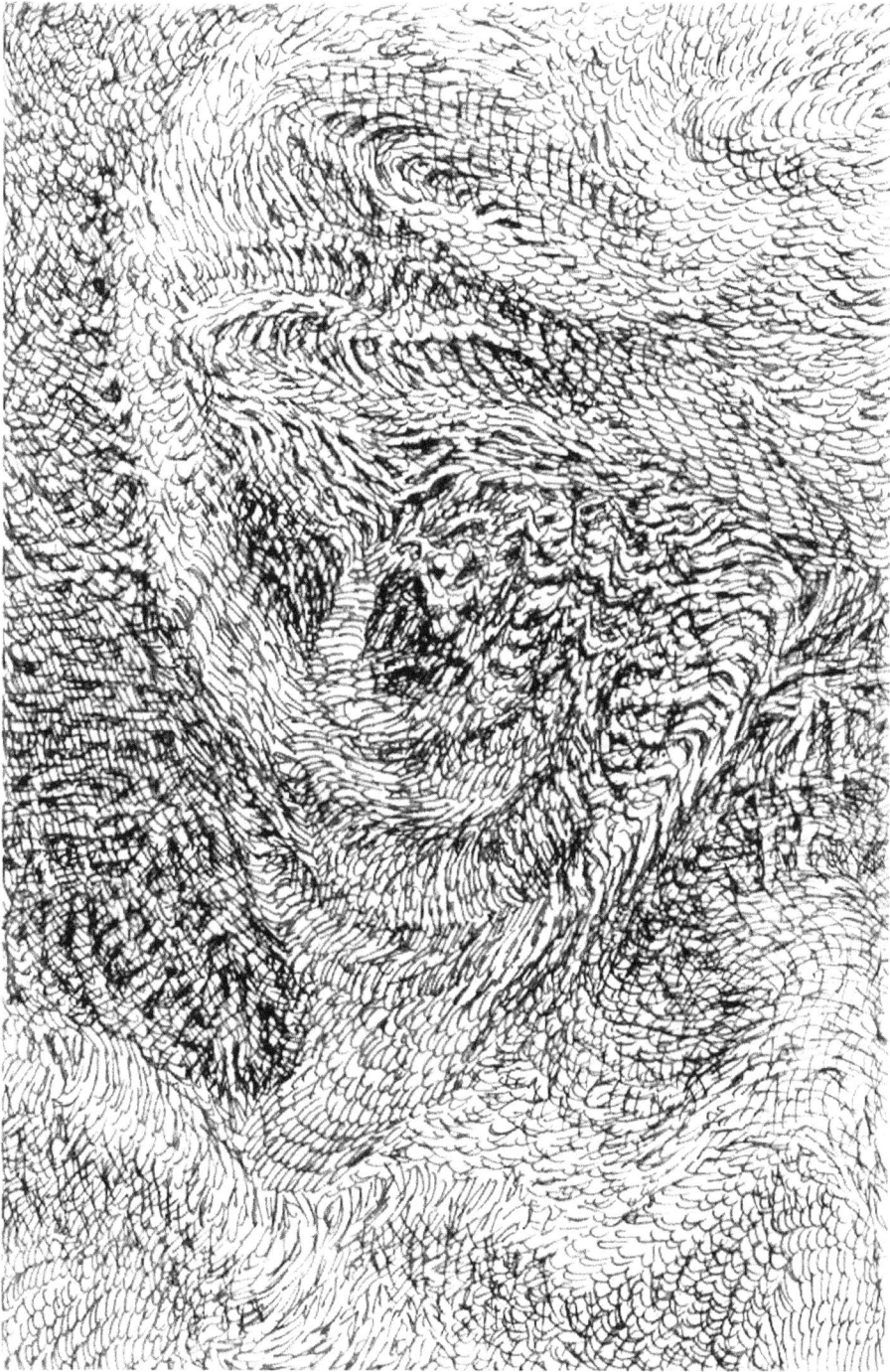

2

On either side of an immaterial table, the kings of silence and the slaves of dialogue give themselves bitterly to the fight. How will they fight? Some kingly, the others slavishly. In this duel, which will be umpired by one of the less compact natures, the slaves have the royal weapons, while the submission skill belongs to the kings.

To begin with, the king of oral thrift is violently silent toward the slave of the method, and sics his drought on a few insolent presumptions that watered him. The slave, who is armed with a verbal sledgehammer, hits him over the fingers, throwing in his eyes a word, which is half-Aramaic and half-Basque. The king withdraws his crushed fingers and weaves with them a long *no* that he throws to the slave in order to silence him. The slave struggles in the *no*'s net; he tries to escape by simplifying it ornamentally, but he's not making any progress and is destroyed.

Now, the slave of the robust argument starts an attack against a taciturn king. He opened the speech floodgates and chatters incessantly like a brutal engine; one hears something like a popping sound ("gombo-gombo") when his voice clashes with the king's inertia. Inundated, defeated by hypotheses and conclusions stated in a liquid, but impersonal, tone, the king will surrender.

Then, a mute king says:

3

Over there (in between the energy woods and the territory invaded by the sliding ruins), the world doesn't have just one up. There is, firstly, an up of smells, from where the miasma descends toward perfume, and down goes berserk. Then, to the right, there is a nocturnal up, always gloomy, through which pass rapidly antinomic ends, and where, periodically, our time self-swallows. Next to it, in the direction 8-10 (if 10 still expresses something, and 8 didn't melt), an elastic up spins some triangular wheels in a certain air. Under it, yet overhead, a rotten up smiles (or smiled; for an up, the present is fluid). Nearby, from the perspective of a choked observer, extends a net of anti-up points, and, in its middle, zenith installed itself.

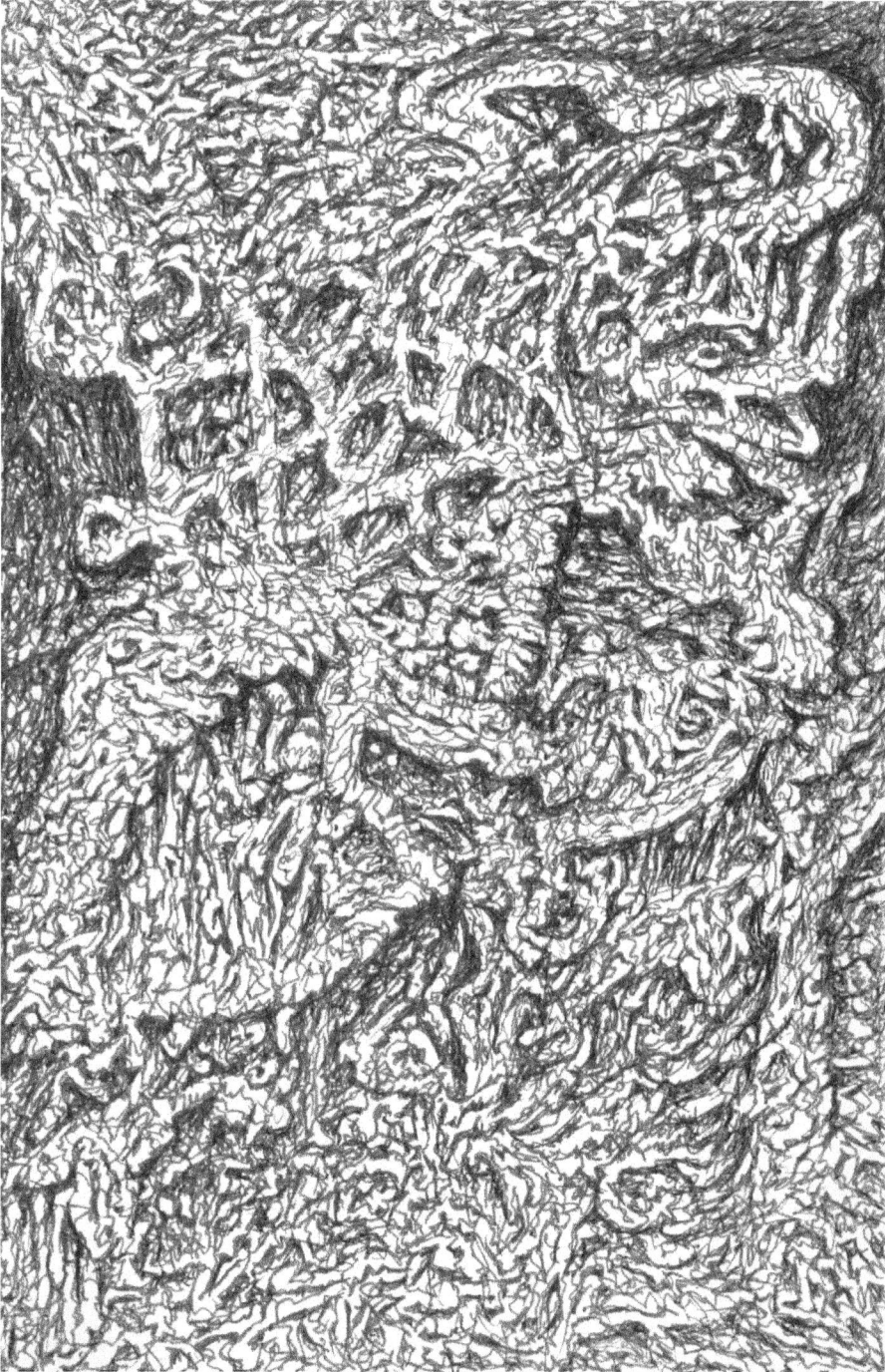

4

Not far from zenith, on some unstable wooden supports that can break at the first light breeze, but don't, the phenomenon expanded. It expanded rapidly (like a blight in a village of dumb giants, where women and billy goats sleep together) and it grew bushy, covering in a few decades a perimeter as big as intracranial France. By growing, it conquered the domains of other similar or opposite phenomena; it scattered their values in chaff and killed their convergence, devouring with a thousand holes the surrounding air and chewing it with enormous mouths.

In one of those mouths, it keeps its fear—in a warm place. It's a slender indoor fear, which would freeze outdoors. Or its tail would stiffen, leaving it with nothing to pound the walls of the phenomenal world, and, gradually, it would grow lazy. Not being pounded by the fear's tail, rhythmically, day by day, the walls that the world created from itself in the proximity of the phenomenon would become permanent. But the phenomenon doesn't want to communicate with such walls; a permanent wall would predispose it to candor.

5

Shy and with both its faces retractile, the tomato grows under the phe-
nomenon. It is a mixture of fibers and echoes united through a fraying
out of the union followed by several coagulating dissipations (like those
of permeable snails, but in reverse). Its two faces—one for action, the
other for mediation—hide a cranium similar to that of felt, which, from
time to time, emits tick-tock insteps in order to regulate its digestion.
(The stomach of the tomato, placed outside its person on a pedestal,
plays only a decorative role: on it there are laid commemorative medals,
ribbons whose taste evokes at times intelligence, and proclamations to
the nation that are read by certain old hags before revolting.)

When the tomato has grown enough, reaching the dimensions of the
Persian Bible, a layer of disparate (but equally intense) meanings cover it,
like a shell.

6

With time, the tomato's shell bursts. It is hit—amiably, but permanently —by the roots of some purple kangaroos, that break and pierce it. The tomato kangaroos are levelheaded polygamists, musicians with an enormous gustatory baggage, and scathing excursionists. In their excursions along attraction fibers, or through the delicate capillary caves formed below time, they like to wet weapons, and they always stop, for one day, at Schenectady, to cool down their flag. (That Schenectady is an itinerant halting-place—one day it's in the USA, another day in Nepal, or on a plate.) When not in excursions, the purple kangaroos stay inside the tomatoes and rotate, each rotation bringing before their eyes a more feudal blood, with aromas of stricken halberds and of yatagans thrust in velvet. This blood has more than one North, and its dispersion on a multi-Nordic plane grants more sacredness in comparison with its southern liquid neighbors, who are always abnormal, always coughing coldly, and ready at any time to set off in search of some elastic sanguine gondolas for transporting their Arabs.

However, for a purple kangaroo, barely issued from a tomato's flesh and with both dimensions weakened, an Arab is a question.

7

Being liquid, for someone from the South, is a duty and a creed. The South (by "South" it is understood a conglomerate of flames) does not allow someone who doesn't flow to climb up. As a devotee, companion, or just a grain of the South, one can flow naturally or, by using flowing pedals affixed to each gush, one can flow forcefully or lazily, torridly, or, on the contrary, coldly (wetting through draining the riverbeds of flowing), but one has, at any cost, to flow. By not flowing, one densifies and disappears.

The flowing peoples have fluvial kings with a rich hydrologic tree, whose tributaries originate from primordial waters. However, a liquid king, unlike a dry one, doesn't resort to coronation in order to establish himself as sovereign. For practical, but also spiritual, reasons, the southern kings renounced the crown as a kingly attribute, replacing it with a star. In the Plantagenet branch, certain stars have golden collars to strangle His Highness with, when he overflows.

8

As forms of flowing toward a paused development, their history is a tu-
bular one: it starts from an impulse of not losing control completely,
goes through some few stages of claws, thorns, or gaping muzzles, and
ends up in an unfavorable emptiness. In the evening, a draft of warm air
passes through the tubes of their history, carrying the melted windows,
the marble that got rotten, the smell of former doors.

9

"Toward calcium!," shouts the leading one (a fierce extrasponge with stripes), and all the living holes—including the western one, who was agonizing timidly—rush toward calcium. The road there goes in between two rows of vertical guts with rushlights on their tops. On each gut, the same emblem: a loaf of bread pierced by arrows, watched by a vulture and a crane, and, between them, on a meadow, the kilogram symbol. In front of the guts, in deep pits, yesterday's bulbs toil on the construction of a subterranean agreement for tomorrow. Is it a breeze that blows softly above, swaying the day, or is it a sigh? We don't know, Aeolus is now nuclear.

Where there is a lot of calcium, there is also a lot of unclear noise. Doors that seem to be slammed in a forest (among trees), a whistling about which one cannot say whether it's matte or shiny, because it starts from a wet biscuit carried on the shoulders of students from a college of champion saints, buzzing of impressions wrapped in a metallic dough (and moaning sometimes, as if they separated reciprocally), howls in fans, from indigo to a guttural yellow, like when one beheads a lamp, volumes of maternal gas that break and release bursts of thousands of sparrows shrieking sharply to announce their emergence, a rain of *Ah* and *Oh* that beats on the ear's window and the ear smiles back, the throb of a hatchet in a galactic mustard before cracking the old order for the stars to arrange themselves differently, and a sigh on a plate, close by.

   Then, for a while, silence. The perforated empires that didn't give in to ascension are retreating in clay, and each one of them is looking for its box.

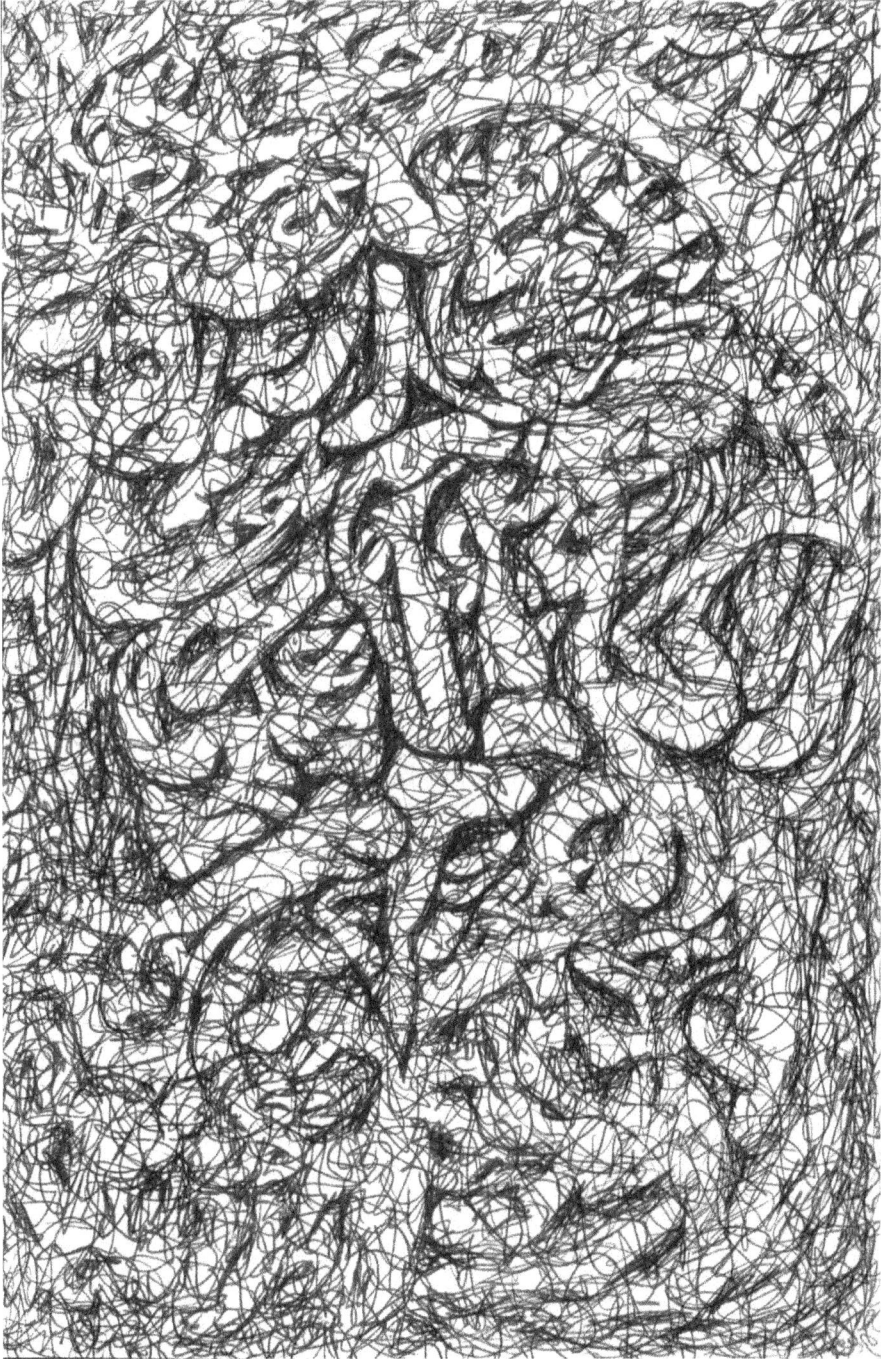

In a completely putrid civilization, as is the civilization of plant teams cultivated in cardboard boxes, enigmas are a social binder. Between two teams situated in the same growth perimeter (the team of Fibers and the team of Petal Weavers, to take just a simple example), the cohabitation relations take the shape of an enigma. Between the cardboard boxes that are the teams' houses, the flow of enigmas is continuous from dawn till dusk, although interrupted for forty-five minutes so that the team members can quench their thirst and clean their thoughts of ashes, resuming afterward for the duration of the night, and reaching its intensity peak around 0:39 o'clock.

Each team member contributes, in turn, to the elaboration of the enigma, using all his abilities and skills. In Fibers' case, Father-Fiber maps out the general framework that will contain the enigma (with fake archways and recesses, open platforms toward bifurcations, and zones of contact with previous or future enigmas), Mother-Fiber fills out that framework with the still formless matter of the enigma (a kind of cheeping clod), and the Sons-Fiber thrust needles (some silvery, some curved, to which they will attach traps) into the matter's crust, to pin it. Once the enigma is ready, one of the younger team members—usually, a dead one—adds a gram of salt to make it supple and hurls it toward their neighbors.

In their cardboard box, seated in a circle, the Petal Weavers wait for it to fall into their arms. And, there—it does. Delighted, they grab its handles and open it up.

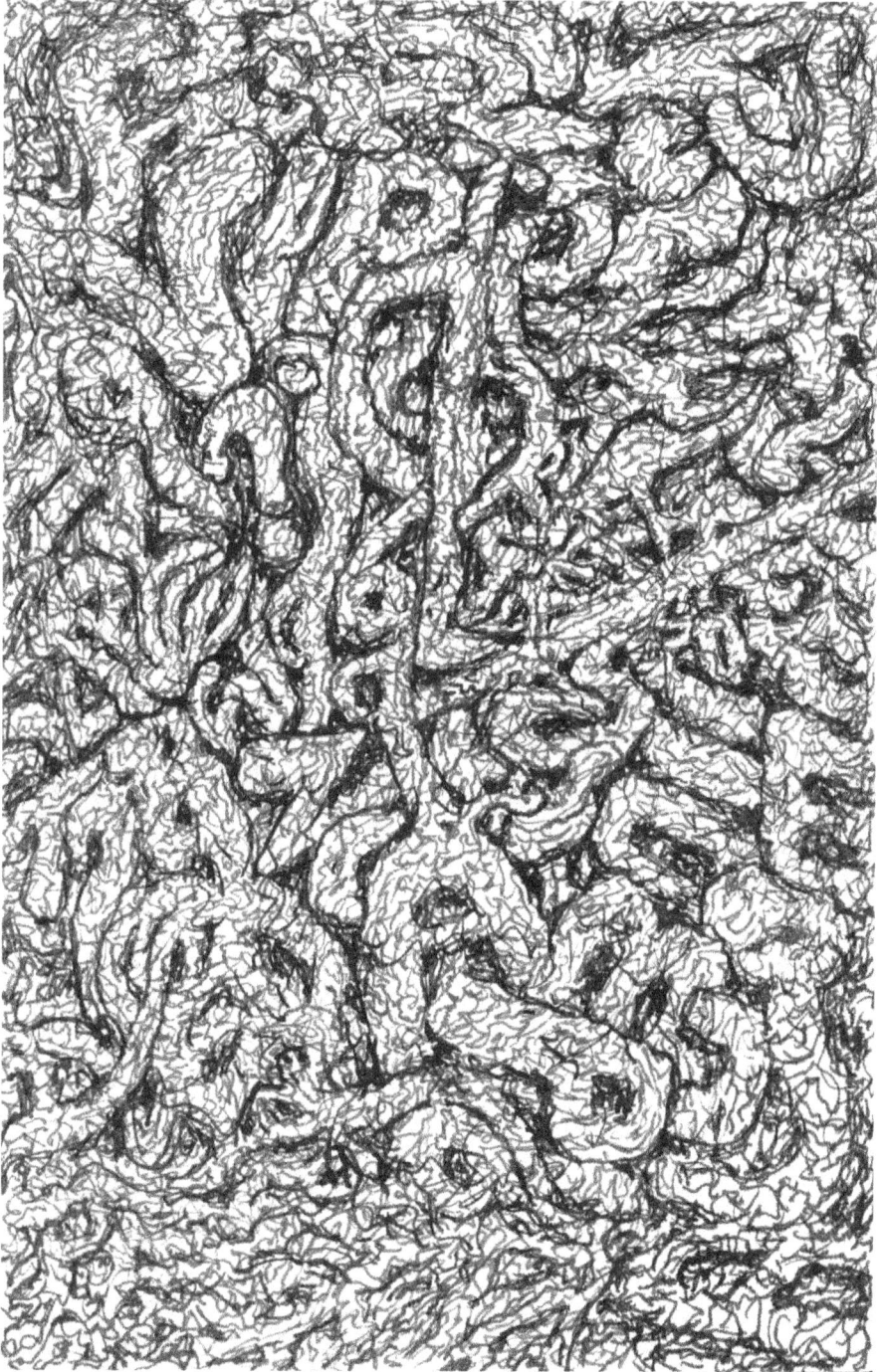

1) *Exuref,* a pedestrian answer (therefore, correct) to the first part of an enigma composed of forty subenigmas, of which eight knotted and one with three answers, each incorrect if taken separately, but exact if taken together. 2) *Gundz,* a mechanical answer (therefore, incorrect) to the twenty-ninth part of the enigma composed of forty subenigmas, of which five got unknotted and three got subdivided in ten infra-subenigmas each. 3) *Olim-clao,* an idiotic answer (therefore, partially correct and partially incorrect) to the eleventh part of the enigma composed of forty subenigmas, for the last six of which the answer is the same *Exuref,* but longer.

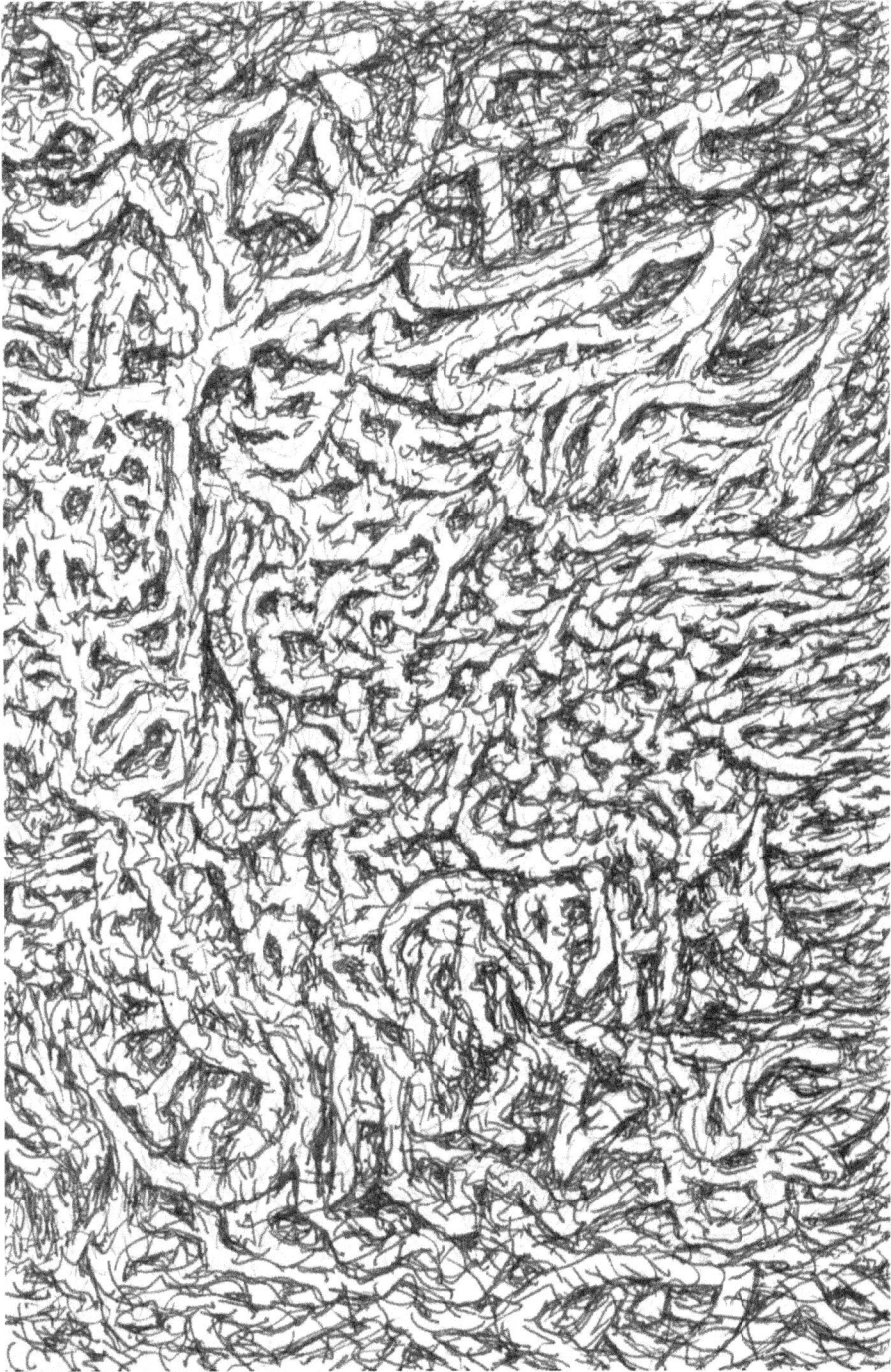

The micro-horse is no docile animal. And it couldn't be otherwise, given that it's but 37% animal, the rest being pure vexation and a drop of amidine.

In order to tame a micro-horse, the teary-eyed cowboys use the power of example. They choose from a box with micro-horses a specimen that is supple, bitter-tasting, and having ironically spiraled hooves (for example, a mustangutan), and throw it into a theologian. The micro-horse recoils (it abhors absorbent theologians), tries to avoid the impact with this recipient of divine mysteries, but falls to its knees. A bridle is immediately put on, and the micro-horse is curried drastically from the days of yore toward the present, molecule by molecule. Defeated, it will leaf out uselessly a few times, and then will obey.

The other micro-horses, knowing by now what awaits them, won't question any conditions.

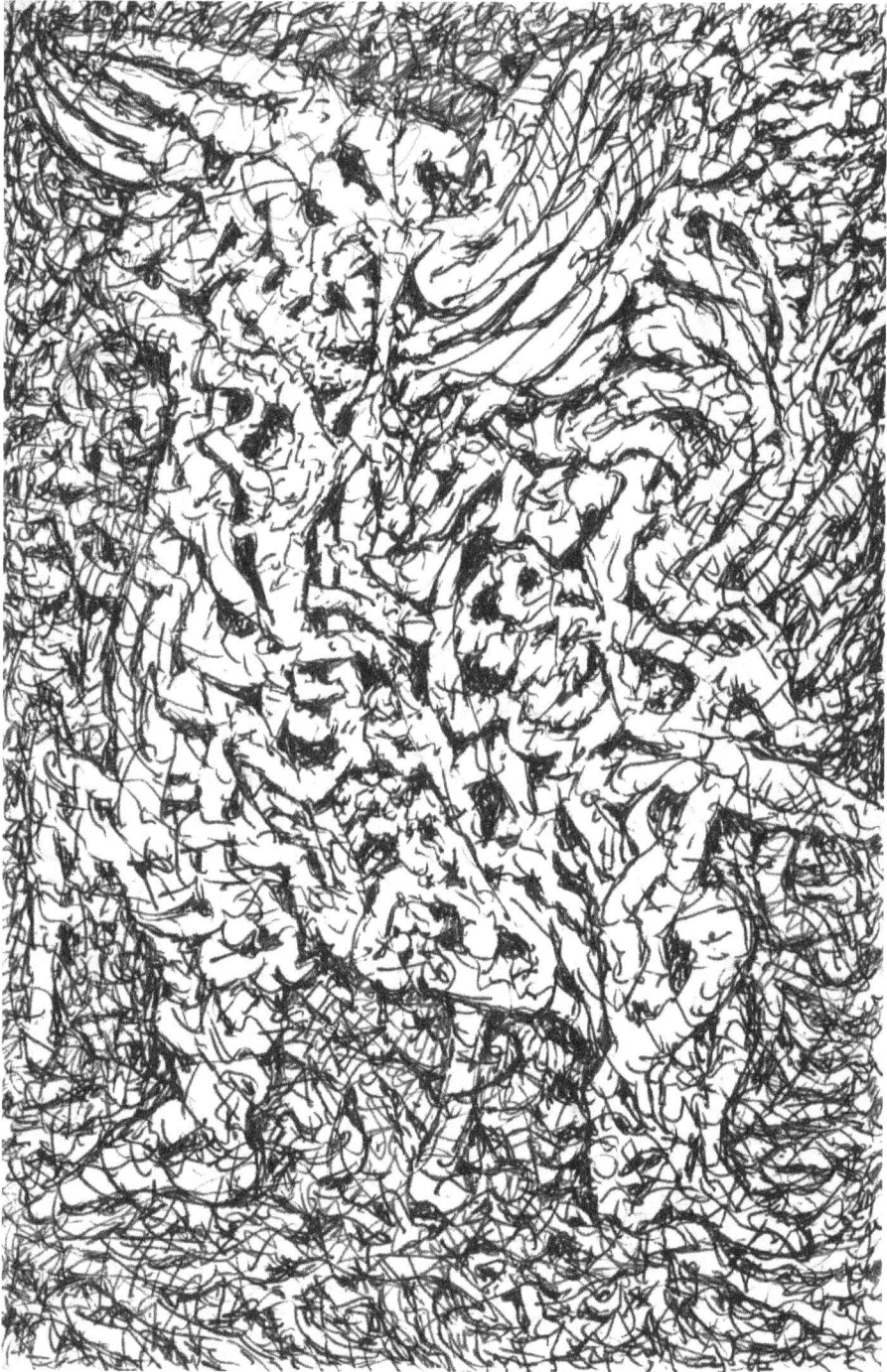

After being tamed, the micro-horses become food for enigmas. Their agitated beauty, having alert contents, is the nourishment that enigmas receive in the evening before heading off toward the realms of sleep. (Regarding the micro-horses' beauty contents, it is believed that their vivacity is due to a supple enzyme, and some say that it saved Robinson Crusoe from the clutches of too slow a digestion. It was in the beginning, when the shipwrecked ate nothing but stones, and sometimes a button.)

The light dims. The day's gates are closed now, between torches and darkness there appear verbal connexions, and gaps are bridged. Astonished by the new smells that enveloped him, a tiger (in a hive, far away) roars. It's the hour of embossed letters written by throwing punches, or built of straw heaps. Ten formulas for the inclusion of the singular in a series, none of them cold enough, come and go on the walls. A micro-horse goes at a walk on a trapeze restrained by someone (or something) not knowing how to wait: a rustling officer, a glory? Upon seeing that, the enigma feels (or thinks that it feels) the thrill of admiration rich in vitamin K. And it falls asleep.

15

Over time, the substance of enigmas thickens, what was vapor becomes canvas, what was quivering aerially starts to settle. Quickly, the hoar ripens in the human trees, building organs, nitrogen honeycombs, peripheral veins, and crusts. The Cube-Sun, radiating more forcefully, coagulates the waters. A basement kite tears up something warm to empty it symbolically, the name of the immature mother is uttered backwards by the clan members, so as not to squander their efforts. Tailored from coldproof materials meant for bad weather, some clothes fill out with bodies.

   That's how the *maestros* appear, not knowing what is going on, how they happen to turn (from mixtures of anomalies) into *maestro* Ether, or *maestro* Colibri.

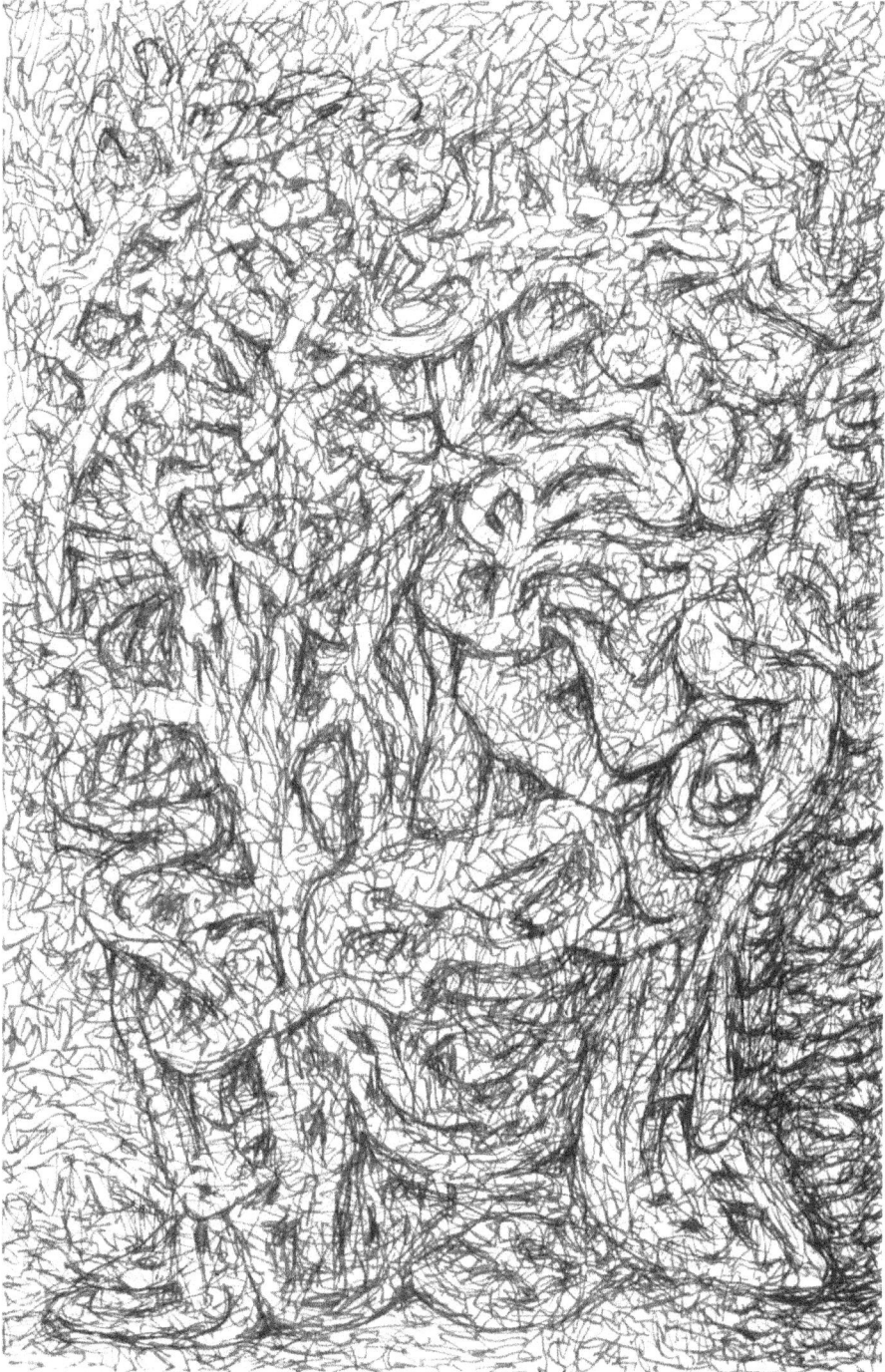

To see *maestro* Colibri disappearing into a body, leaving one world and passing into the flesh of another (where Extants can coexist nutritiously with Inextants) is a rare thing. Not because an Extant like *maestro* Colibri would like to hide somehow his disappearances (on the contrary, he wants them extremely public, and, if possible, known worldwide), but because he disappears by blinding you. An observer, who would be present, wittingly or unwittingly, at the scene, would notice only a snap. To a degree, it's natural: the assimilation of the Extants by the Inextants is a cruel process, that could be softened by the presence of witnesses.

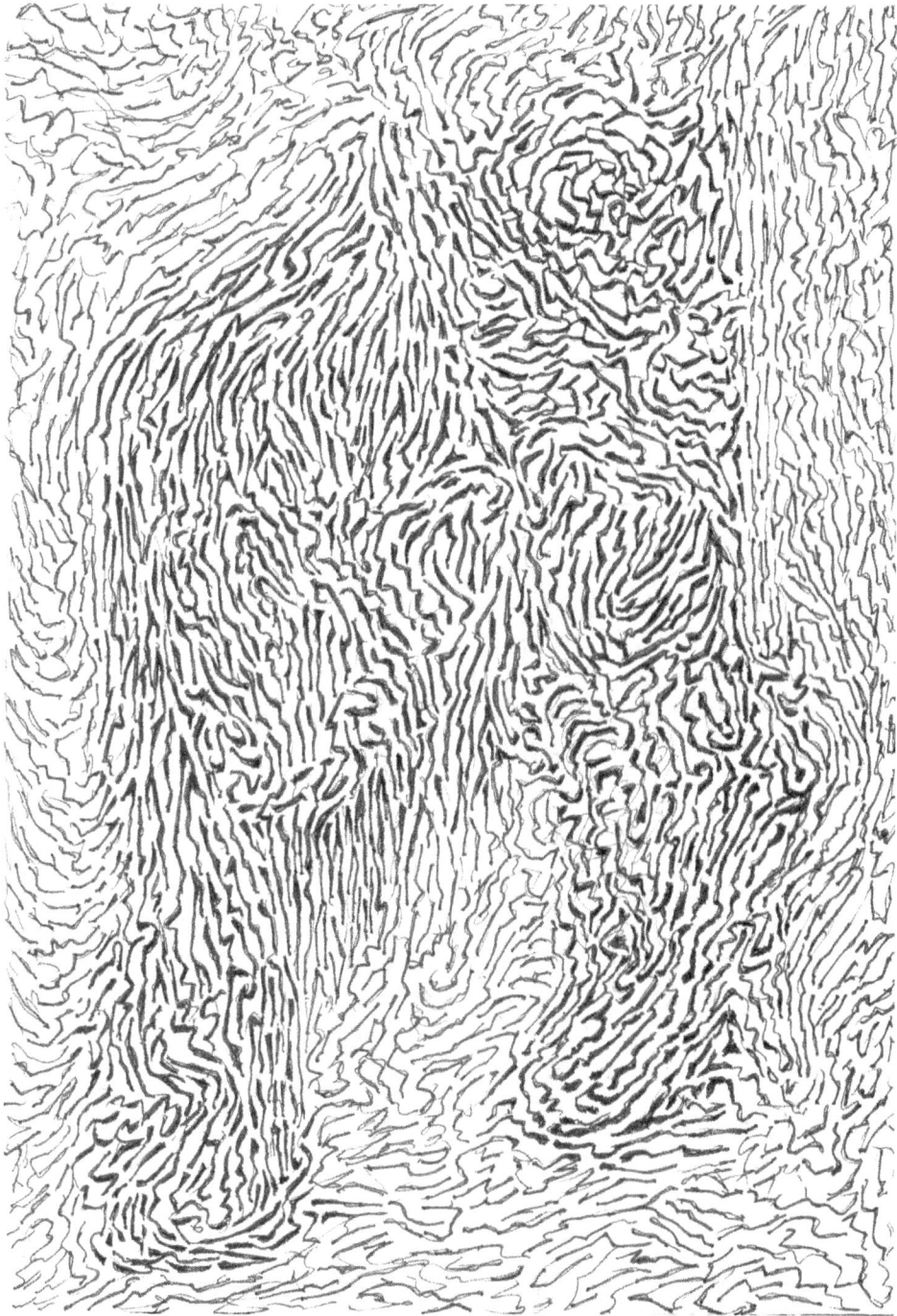

It says "Approved" in raised letters on the sole of the only shoe that *maestro* Colibri is wearing. His other feet don't need shoes: the second is bare to the bone, the third and fourth retreated into his hips, the seventh and the eighth replaced walking with magnetic accidents. But what about the fifth and the sixth?

Fortunately, they ublak anteonolla.

18

For someone like *maestro* Colibri, each of his actions, each of his gestures, and each of the thoughts that cross his mind must have a fraudulent character. In the morning (under an incomplete beltless Sun), the *maestro* awakes from his sleep (what a night! what a storm of emotions! what abyss!) exhausted. He pushes aside the night vapors (seven vapors with illustrious names), but keeps two of them for later examination in the tramcar. He swallows (the torch lights up in his throat) a few shark seeds stolen from a shop where only old penknives, with bellows, are sold. As an echo of the persistence of certain filial hooks, he hugs his wall-mother, telling her how bitterly he loves her (shoulders are tinkling). And so, he goes to sing in an isolated tower, where nobody can hear how his voice is breaking.

His Agora is a humble turf taken from the wig of a former pharmacy, now closed in order to regain its grandeur. It's there that he had gathered his fear, and now he stretches its linens, covering, whitening, or covering in cruel clothes his need for noise.

It's clear: *maestro* Colibri has a way of being, which is totally fraudulent.

The nocturnal vapors Emoria and Leblanc interweave dreams. Emoria takes the red ones (with animals, heavy tools, or anonymous individuals who intervene brutally on the ego) while Leblanc takes the black ones (the so-called Vehiculum dreams, in which one waits). The rhinoceroses, followed closely by elephants and egrets, appear constantly in the dreams that Emoria spins for weaving with the dreams spun by Leblanc. This is called—using a technical term, for lack of a better one—the "rhinoceros constant." In Leblanc's case, it's the opposite—in the dreams that he spins, something rarely appears.

Example: you made a date at 8 o'clock, in a square, with a gray woman, of which you were told that she would have bow qualities, in order to solve together the harmony problem. While waiting for her, you examined carefully a series of terms printed here and there on rocks, or in the clouds' movement, deciphering some, some others not. At 9 o'clock, when you were ready to fade away, she would come toward you accompanied by a cute rhinoceros, and thus you would be able to recognize her more easily.

Images from apartments that appear in red dreams (these images were drawn by the vapor Emoria, with drops on a towel): in apartment 2, a Catholic deep sea diver kneeling in the bathtub to ask the water for forgiveness; in apartment 18, the sacrificing of a virgin oak tree, in a simulacrum of profanation of decency (or of christening?); in apartment 18B, two leaves in embrace on a napkin next to a study on aromatic numbers; in apartment 23, nothing (although in flames); in apartment 29, a box, in the box, a cube, in the cube, a sword that got wilted; in apartment 30A (after Ampère A), three walls covered in pizza dough, and, on the fourth, a painting, out of which a lazy Missouri is flowing; in apartment 36, three Latvian esthetes (one myopic, the other ones on crutches) admiring, among other things, a beginning; in apartment 71 (the only one that fits on a sailing ship), a few anchors hanging from the ceiling, under them, a mattress, and on the mattress, the trophies—algae and blood.

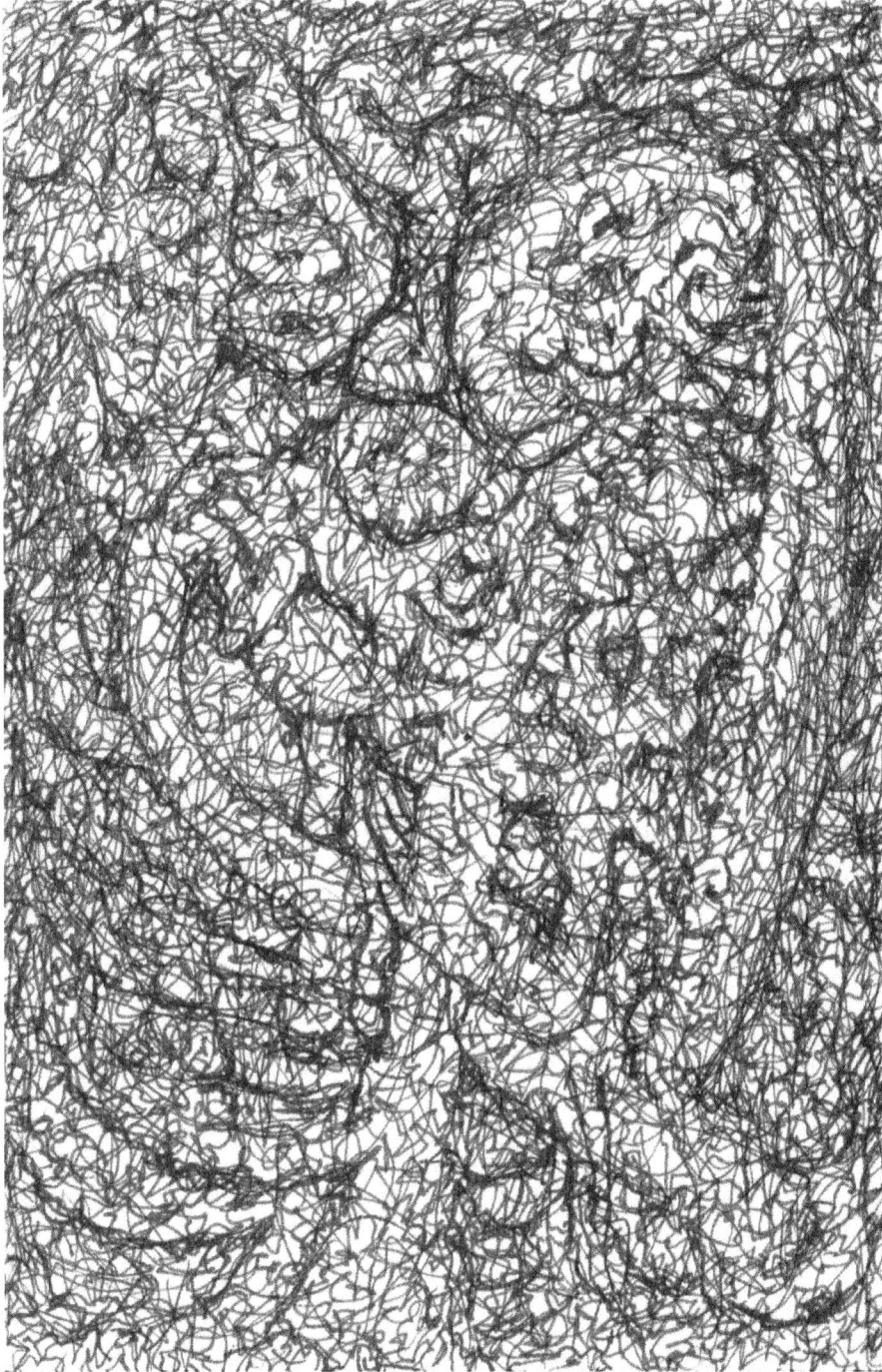

Sometimes (but very seldom), in Vehiculum dreams one can see a few fibers. Actually, the person who dreams rather feels than sees them, because their apparition in the lower left part of the dream doesn't retain one's attention: a glimmer, a quick rustle, and the fibers disappear. By the time one realizes what kind of fibers they were and what they were doing there, the dream has taken other paths, leaving them behind. However, an experienced dreamer knows how to proceed in such instance. He hits the brakes, rewinds the dream slowly (as to not cause the silver layer to evaporate), and stops at the fiber scene. He bends down to the lower left corner, where the dream is covered by a cloth, then lifts it (without naming it), or tears it. He sees the fibers. More precisely, he sees a group of ballerina fibers thinking of a certain thing. "Aha," he says, and resumes his dream, now knowing what he is dealing with.

When thinking fibers appear, however sporadically, in a Vehiculum dream, they are the sign of a deep ascension, or of an impasse.

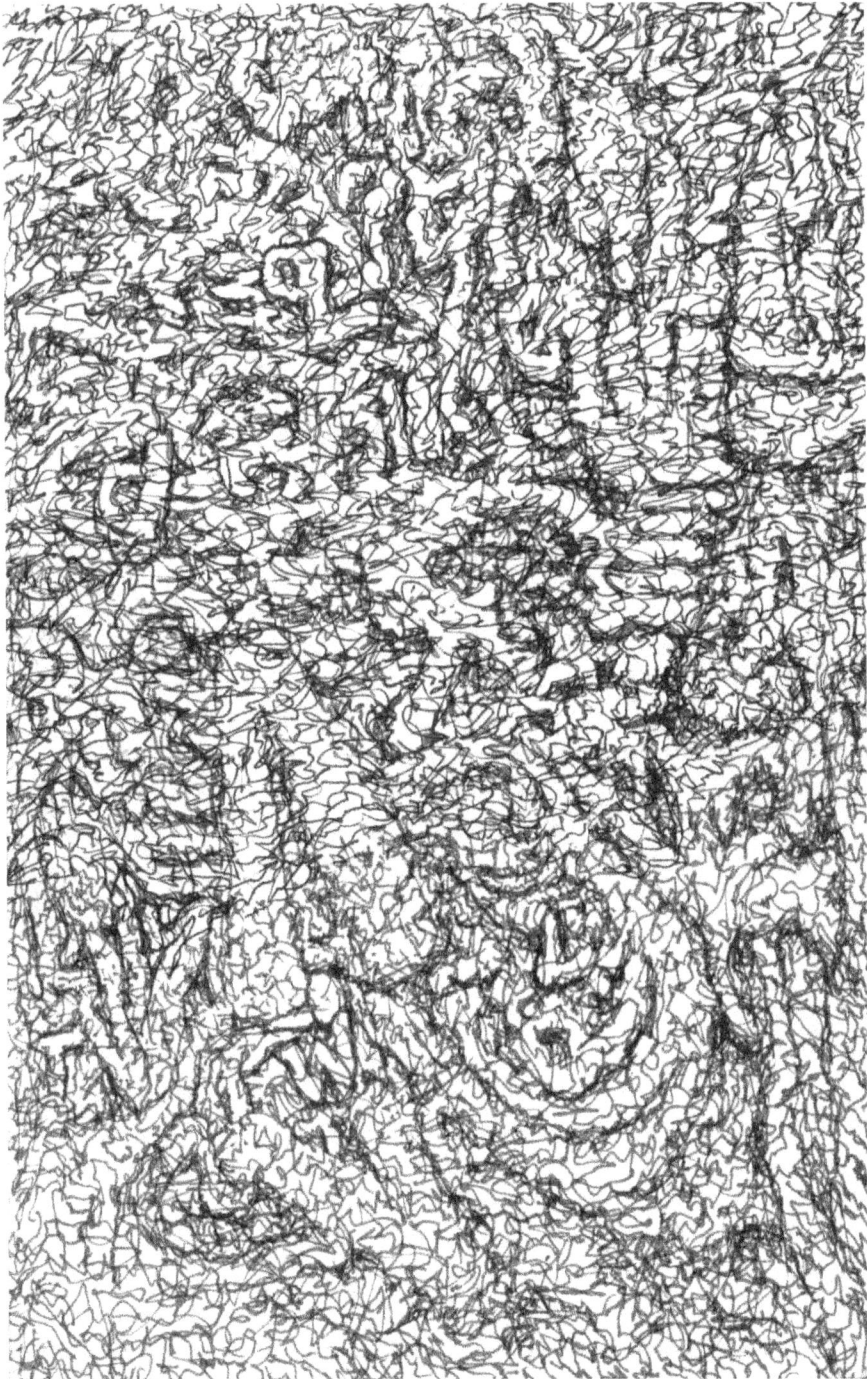

Among the species of thinking fibers, the peaceful fibers (with only two warriors for a population of eight hundred people) are the only ones who adopted the undulatory thinking. If in the case of other fibers their thinking track can be represented schematically through a straight line (or a broken line, in the case of ballerina fibers), in the case of peaceful fibers it looks like a row of curls. Some curls exhibit an abrupt, even dizzying, roundness, if thinking is in ebulition, while other curls' roundness is milder, if thinking sprawls.

 A sprawling thinking, whose curls barely give a start when touched by the breeze of an idea, is no less lively than one that is flaring and foaming. In a way, its curls are as active as when boiling, but with reduced efficiency expenditure, which to the fibers appears to be essential, in order not to get exhausted.

Rebel fibers, who are the slowest of the fibers, took a few millennia to develop the art of the tumble. The first step (after having agreed on the idea of a tumble, and on the advantages that it would bring to the group) was choosing a suitable color, which should have been neither a color of ecstasy (because ecstasy fattens), nor one of lack of energy (energy is liked by everyone). They chose, by voting with flags, a sublime greenish gray.

Then, for seven generations, they filtered it to separate the impurities (remains of cold, cautious looks, or pirouettes of doubt), and to extract the essence of a diffuse greenish gray. This gray was to define their tumble, distinguishing it sharply from the other tumbles belonging to other fibers.

Three centuries and fifteen years passed until the rebel fibers came to a decision regarding the extent of the tumble. Throb or leap? A fourth degree rotation with sparks, a simple rotation with down, or a non-rotation with waves? Swirl, whirlpool, or vortex? Needle-, or mirror-like? Followed by a plus, or a minus? From the elliptical toward the ambiguous, or not? Through a vote with leaves they decided in unanimity that it would be a broken travel. (The travels that one brakes, the same as the stroll of a dull individual along the thread of his life, have the advantage of being incoherent.)

Having clarified this, the fibers rested for the following thousand years. (Fiber years, it has to be said, don't have duration, but only height and, sometimes, weight.) Now and then, in order to revive their dialectics, they would vote again (with meteorite fragments, snuffed candles, or anything else) on how to begin the tumbles. Should they do it in whispers, so that the tumble god wouldn't hear them and ask whether they had any approval? Or should it be noisily, by singing a manual song? They didn't come to an agreement then, during their thousand-year rest, but later, in the eighth millenium of reflection and debates.

They were exhausted (some of them were surprised to be still alive), and the first tumble of the rebel fibers was a swoon. One of those big swoons that spin the world, a splendid greenish-gray swoon.

Between two tumbles, rebel fibers produce forests. It's an activity at rest, which doesn't imply the effort of renouncing the sitting position, and doesn't require too big an expense of quietness. Practically, in order to produce a forest, it's enough for a green ego to touch a blonde ego. Or for a thin ego to be touched by the rear end of a wide ego. Upon touching, the fibers' egos flinch and separate from the carrier fiber, becoming thus independent. The blonde ego (which resembles a mechanical prince perforated by butterflies in black suits) bends over the green ego (a kind of stepless wheel), and opens it. Several blurry embroideries spring out at the first eruptions, becoming clear, however, after the parallel emergence principle is abandoned. From those embroideries appear hands holding burning torches, and each and every torch roars when the clay drips. It dripped completely? The torches emptied out to the last drop? Then the whole valley fills up with trees.

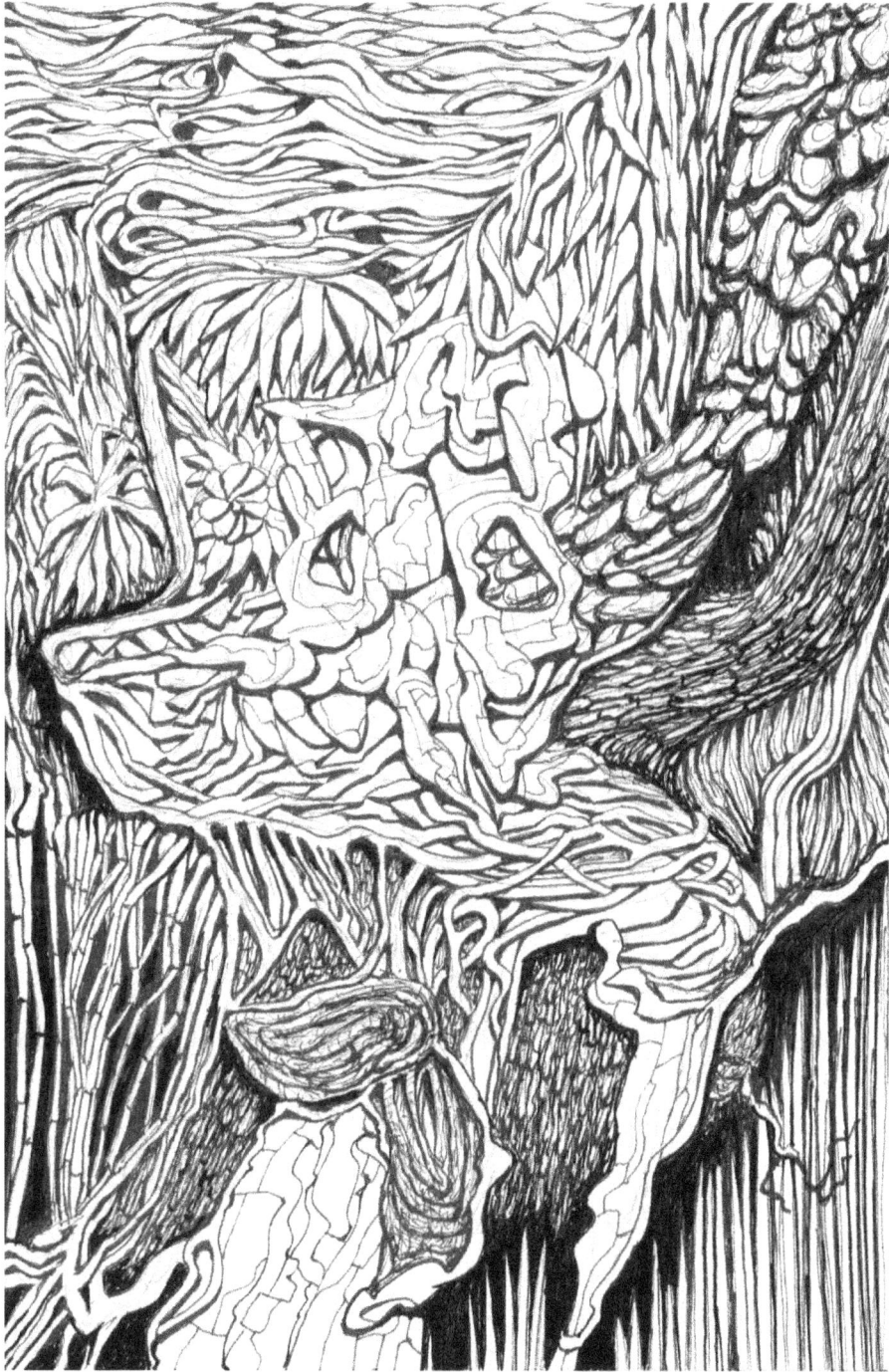

The forest-shell appeared from the need of some trees to contemplate their tops. Conifers, especially, a profoundly contemplative tree species that spend up to twelve hours per day contemplating their own trunks, would have liked to have the forestry equivalent of a mirror, in order to admire their upper parts, which are inaccessible to their ever-horizontal gaze. Among conifers, the chameleon-pine, the fir with a fan and the midday spruce fir were the most fierce contemplators, so fierce that sometimes they would get lost in the contemplation abyss, from where only the iron arms of certain ferns could extract them. Unfortunately, before the forest-shell could solve this problem, there were registered a few cases of fir trees that couldn't be saved—they would disappear for-ever in that personal inside, from where one gets out only with great difficulty.

In order to put an end to those unwanted losses, the chieftains of the tree tribes decided to import seashells, their proclivity to reflect being a known fact. More than that, if one rustles in their vicinity, they think of themselves as mirrors. In exchange for a branch and four pine cones, a trader-plant from the network of shrubs for profit, delivered to the forest a pair of adult seashells, that acclimated perfectly among trees. From time to time, toward dusk, after the spruce trees have examined closely the splendor of their tops and have retreated in meditation, the seashells sigh.

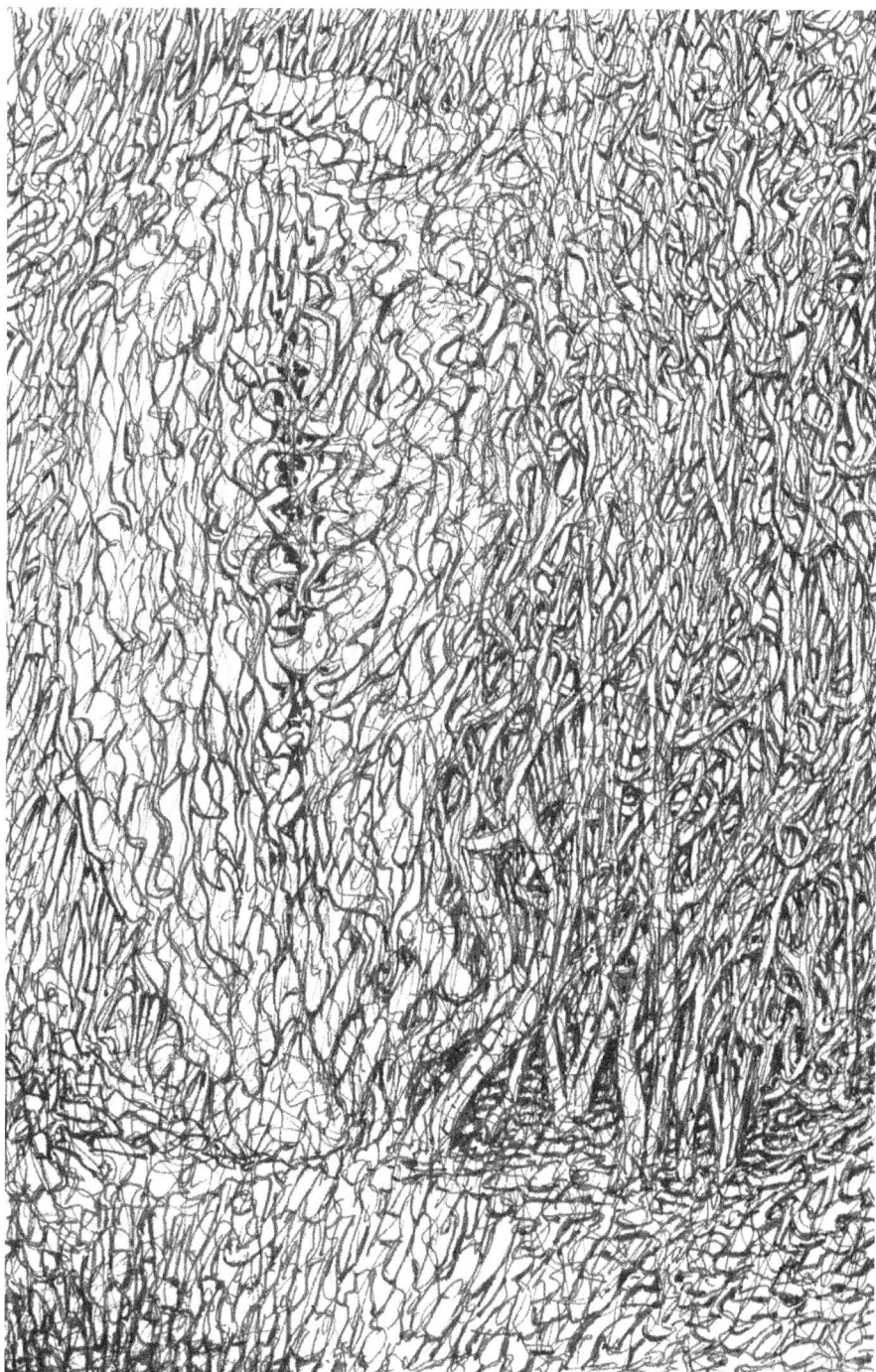

26

It seems that in hay, bearing balls and shark fat there were found identical particles arranged either in free chains (in hay's case), in oscillating pyramids (in bearing balls' case), or in couples of eights (in sharkfat's case). These particles—named for now "Gojo particles," after the name of a dog that was passing through the lab when they were discovered—have a ceremonious-aberrant behavior and become luminescent when in contact with vinegar. Coupled up, they branch out in series of indifferent Gojo particles, their indifference serving them as amphitheater, or, in cases of green coupling, as lamp post. Thus, the coupling of a chain of Gojo particles with a pyramid of Gojo particles (oscillating lazily) produces a spherical hay so indifferent, that its light absorbs any rustle.

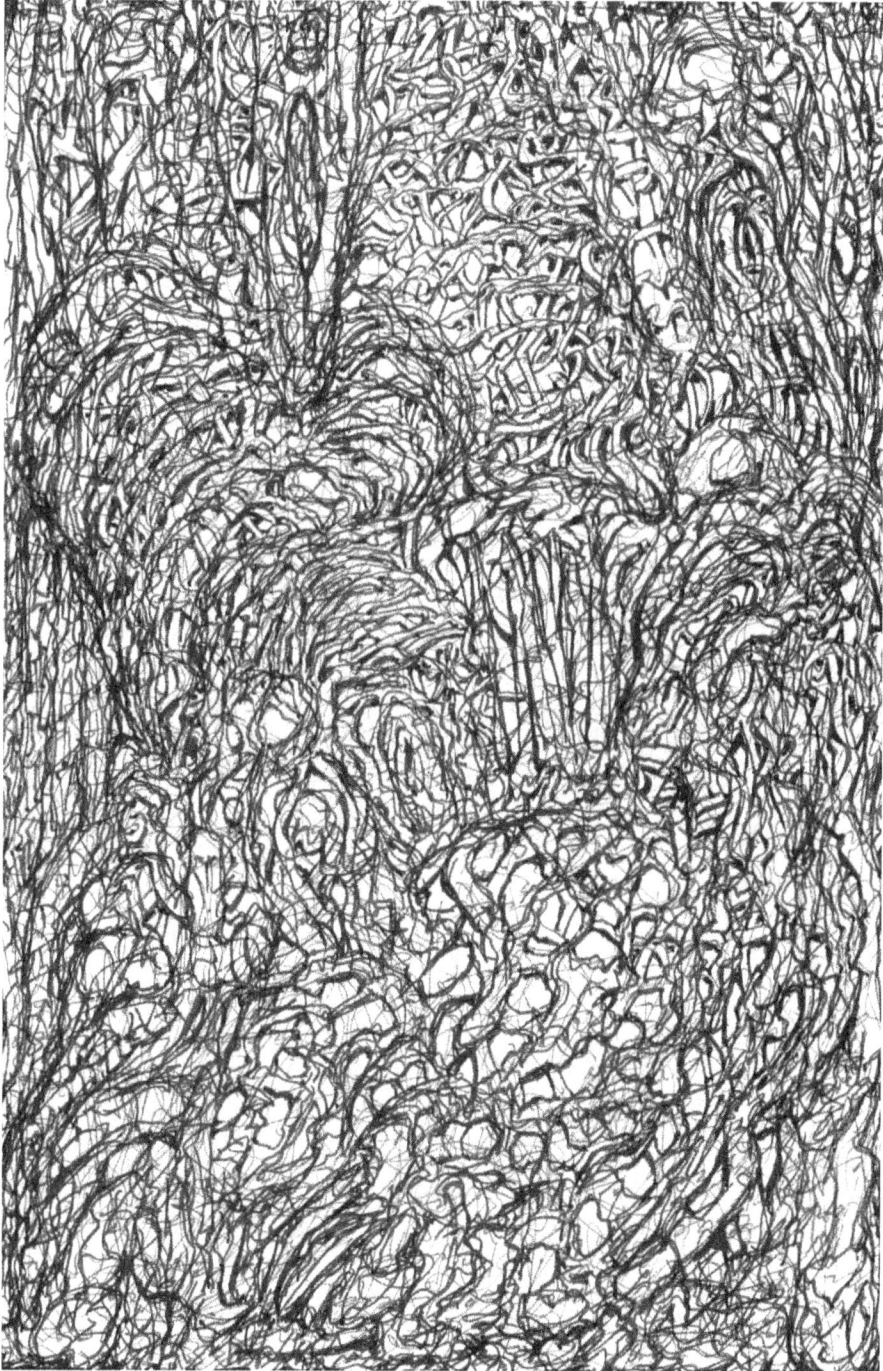

27

A subcategory of the indifferent Gojo particles consists of the impossible Gojo particles ("impossibles," for short), which are present in the composition of conversation knives and in certain varieties of coal, such as the osseous coal. Their mode of organization has nothing to do, as it was believed at one time, with placing stars on a canvas (whichever it may be), but rather with the adapting of an uncertain scheme to an unstable frame. In order to pin what is to be pinned, and to leave the alternative in motion, one more thing has to be said: the "impossibles" can.

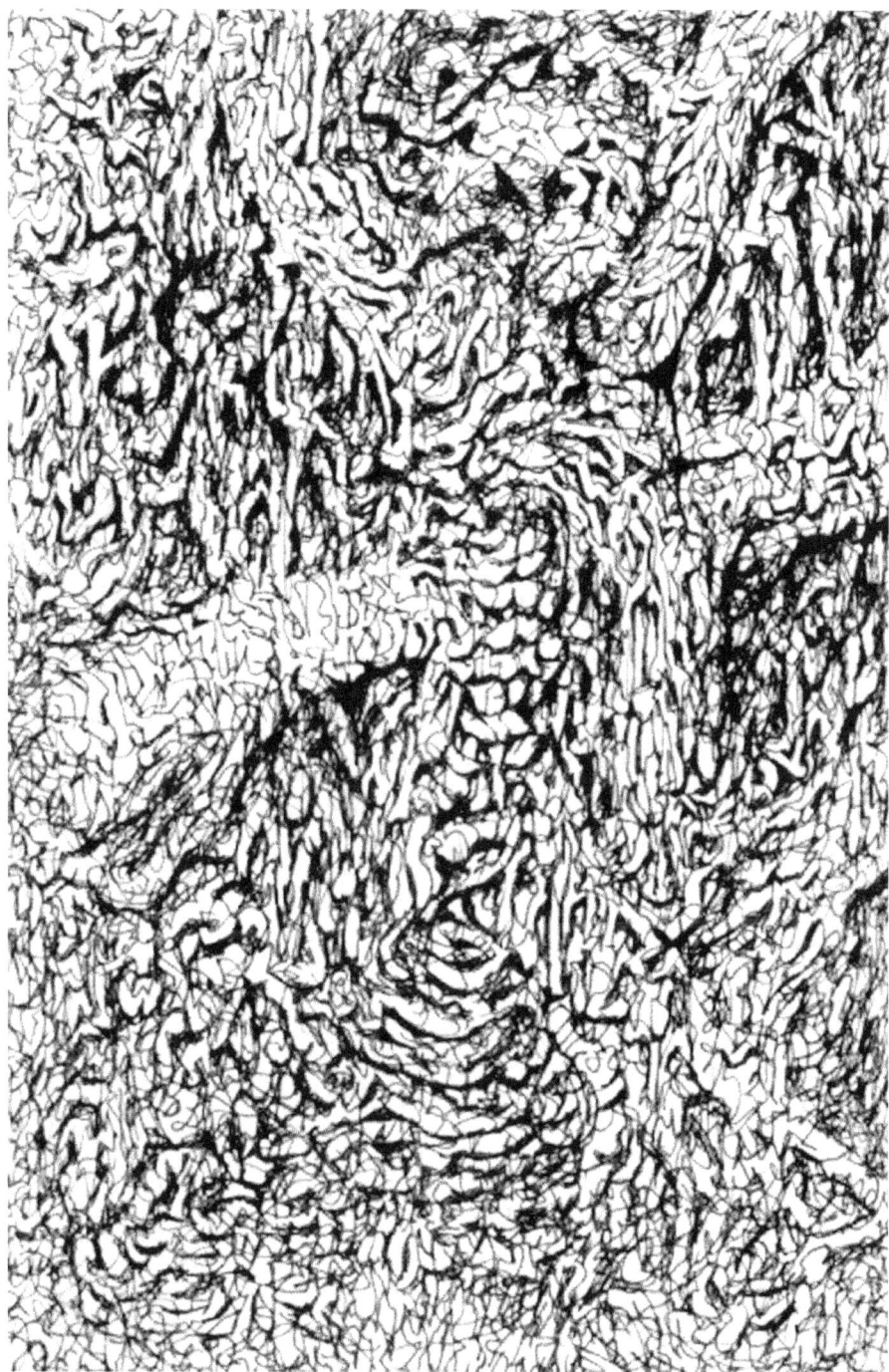

28

Two of the "impossibles" ("impossible" 3 and "impossible" 3F) go through periods when they feel electric, each in its own way, and produce refusal. Refusal, in the world of the impossible Gojo particles' subcategory, is what honey is in other worlds. If in that world there would be teaspoons (or at least some slow connections in the shape of teaspoons), all the atoms therein, even those refractory to sweetness, would like to taste a spoonful of refusal in the evening.

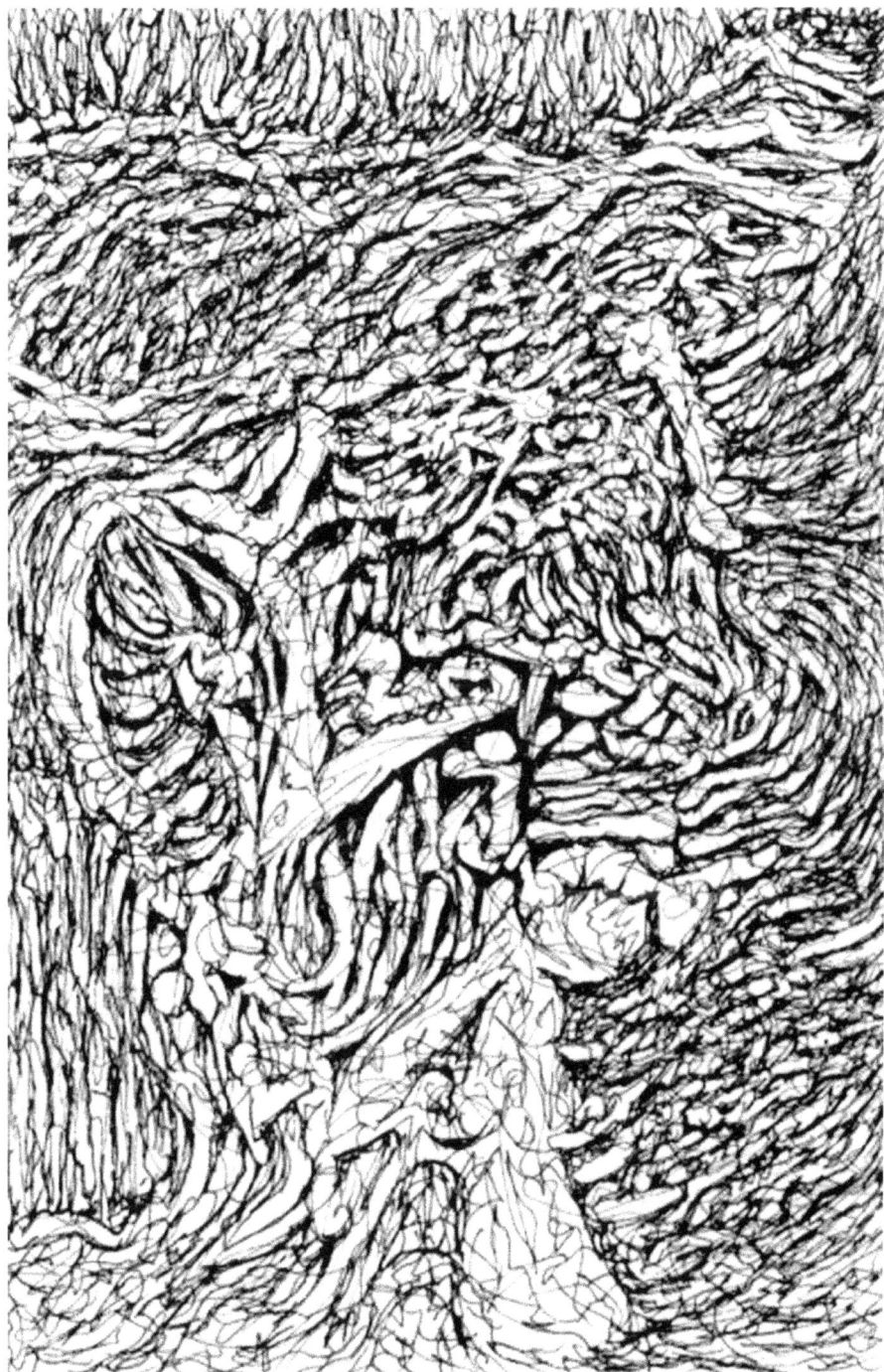

29

When they don't feel electric, "impossible" 3 and "impossible" 3F produce sanctity. They produce it by ticking, squeeking, or whizzing, depending on the texture of the sacred nourishment that they have to digest. The sanctity produced by ticking gave to faith a series of always exact saints, guided by a straight rigor on the hard road of selflessness. Among them, the most prominent in exactness was Saint Bandage, the first martyr of precision, protector of shy people and of those afflicted by sadness. Sanctity produced by squeeking generated a multitude of saints too, albeit approximate ones: Saint Lightbulb, Saint Back Pocket, Saint Mud, or the Saint Alaskan Varices, worshipped (and given offerings) by those who are too lonely. Lastly, to the sanctity produced by whizzing, one can attribute only Saint Fixa, whose bone relics, touched in passing with one's shoe, are a cure for shooting pains.

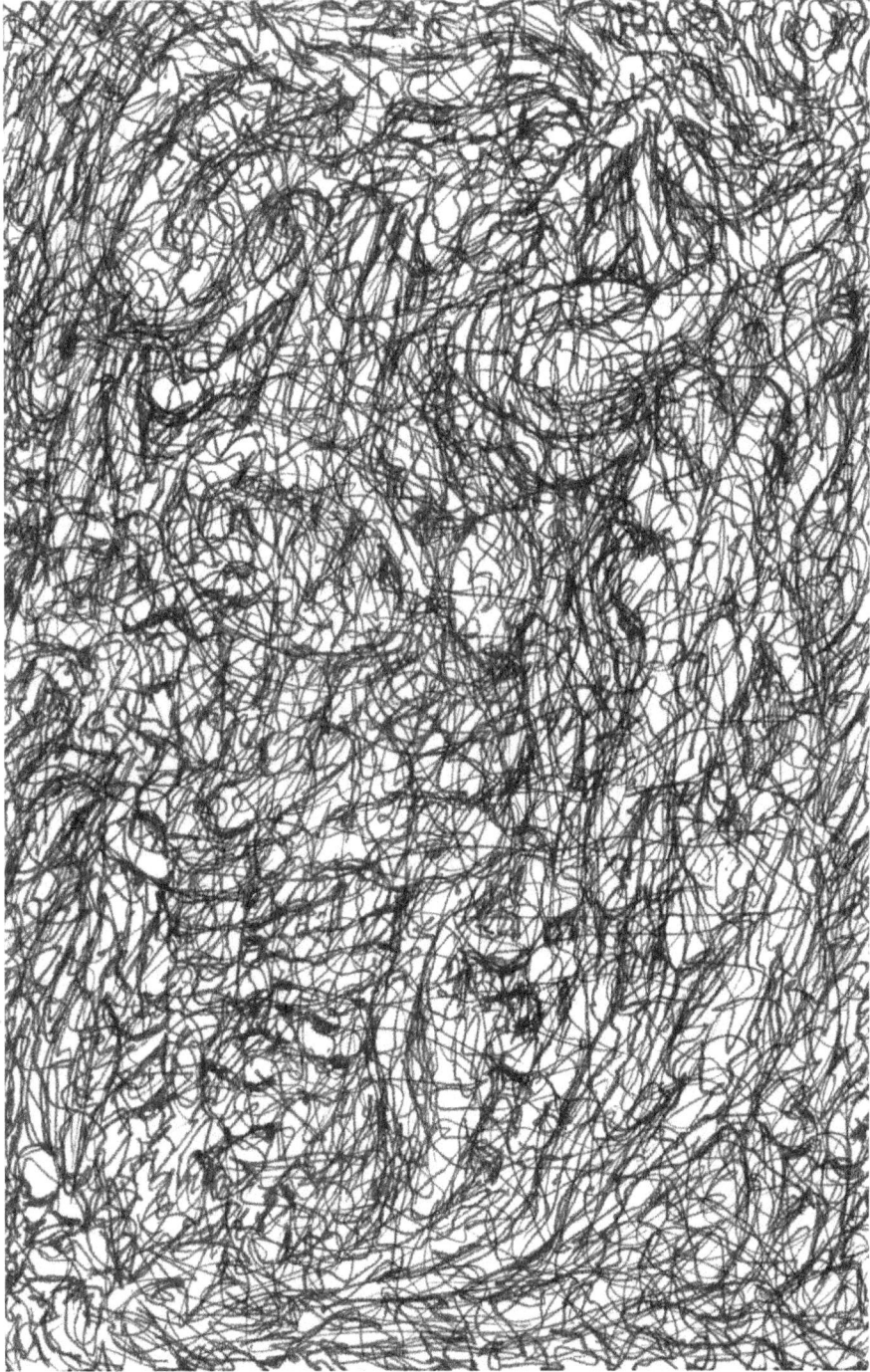

30

In Vehiculum dreams, since they are black, there appears nothing that we know. There appear lines (if we can call "line" a non-tall, but oblong, body), round noises like the mouth-larva, but with brush-teeth, mottled human mosaics from zones of flesh alternating with zones of something else, a kind of living nets (or only living their weaving), out of which pour fish, white clouds in loose dresses with networks of tubes on their shoulders, heavy shadows, of which one diminishes, while the others swell or stretch, muta-genic exemplars of a species of rudimentary pliers adapted only to walking in a convoy, to night thinking and to the absence of any purpose, volumes shaken by a spasm, relatives of some digits burned in a vessel, who arrived to kindle a river in their memory (they wrote on the water's surface *R.I.P.* in letters of chlorine), oceanic carpenters sawing boards while swimming, strangers of ours (one recognizes them by their locusts) mixing our time with theirs, pumps for taking out clay from veins when someone crumbles and has no place to freeze, avid holes, pits with tumulus voices, infra-supremes, columns in a pilgrimage (to the reliquary of Saint Fixa), whose only fuel is a yeast, sayings in narrow vestments of anathemas with a grin above the ankle to tread greenly, standard-bearing ravens, flocks of pitchforks driven toward illusory jacuzzis, where haste is waiting for them, pumpkins running every which way from the path of released zebras, slow foams in a nimble space, balloons tasting like children, three nenuphars on a simple mountain.

31

Vibratile scaffolding surrounds, like a muff of brushwood, the body of the Saint Curtain Cathedral. On the scaffolding, microscopic workers (who are unobservable, or observable with difficulty by a sullen observer) raise reed fences modeled after bras with paddle wheels. These fences, somewhat living and built in such a way that they can bolt at any squeak of a bell, will be the guardians of mammary altars, from where the Curtain priests, donning fluted Galilean cassocks and wearing on their heads the abstract birdcages of the Sacred Meter, will splash the multitude of followers with drops of joy.

(A sacred meter has a hundred centitears.)

32

Before drying in the sun on the night when the "impossible" 3 and "impossible" 3F produced three ounces of refusal, Fixa (whom the drying and a whizzing tick-tock have turned into a saint) was one of the servants of Saint Curtain. Her duty was to keep clean, regardless of the consequences, the skin of her mistress. Saint Curtain didn't show her skin in the world, on fishtank-boulevards or in the markets where toreador organs are sold, but kept it hidden in one secret chamber of her body, known to her close ones as the "Chamber of my Skin," where only Fixa had access. She entered there using a blind key that she turned in the eye of a marsh.

When the marsh would open (squeeking and coughing liquidly), before Fixa appeared the skin's expanse of pores. Each pore was an amphora dripping seductions, some almost clear, others dirty or darkened by the time's embrace. At one end, the skin would wind on an anti-wrinkle reel, which smoothed it and restored its splendor once a year, in winter. The other end, free, would hang above the Curtain's internal waters, a lot of them cold.

As a vestal with full powers of Saint Curtain, Fixa didn't have a lot to do inside. She would light a memorial fire in a vulture (who sat, its wings spread out, on a broken globe, looking closely at some kind of nothing) and would wait for the fire to consume it. Then, she would spray the surface of the skin with whitening gas, cathedralizing it.

33

On Gazelle Days, a procession of industrial ghosts, butlers of the Infra lords and sour Dulcineas pass by, carrying on their shoulders (or on the cables of their shoulders) Fixa's bones. The retinue stops at each bridge for the bones to have their shadow adjusted, and to be touched, with a fish, by the fishermen. (The contact between fish and bone, through which the fish information is transmitted to the bone, is a step toward the eighth resurrection, the one that will return Fixa to breathing.)

Other touchings happen in places unfrequented during the day, where the attendants are deprived of their protection organs and their eyes get shut. When they emerge from there, they don't have the same sight (they see only simple lines), and the bones that they carry have gotten heavier.

Almost alive, Fixa asks for—and is given—the Quantity.

34

What makes Saint Curtain's skin different from other equally complex skins is its *selective tangibility*, a quality that allows it to be touched only by certain fingers. If an unwanted finger gets too close, trying to examine it, rejection weapons jump out of the skin and freeze the intruder. It's not unusual to see around there hands (hung above weak fires, or crawling in the grass) with four, three, or two fingers—some even with one. Those are unimportant hands, that wouldn't have benefited sensitively the skin by touching it.

There is, naturally, a hierarchy of fingers that are allowed to wander freely on certain stretches of the skin, and not all of them have access everywhere. On shoulders are accepted the flap-fingers (adept with the needle), that sew what is to be sewn in order to prepare the subcanvas. Subcanvases are dealt with by the string-fingers, admitted in the region of the thorax and at the joints, but barred from the throat. Only the funnel-fingers can get there, during the pauses for voice changes, clearing it by emptying the coagulated saliva, and moistening its words. Only one spike-finger gets to the cheek, where the Curtain's skin creases radially, and requires to be palpated from the inside.

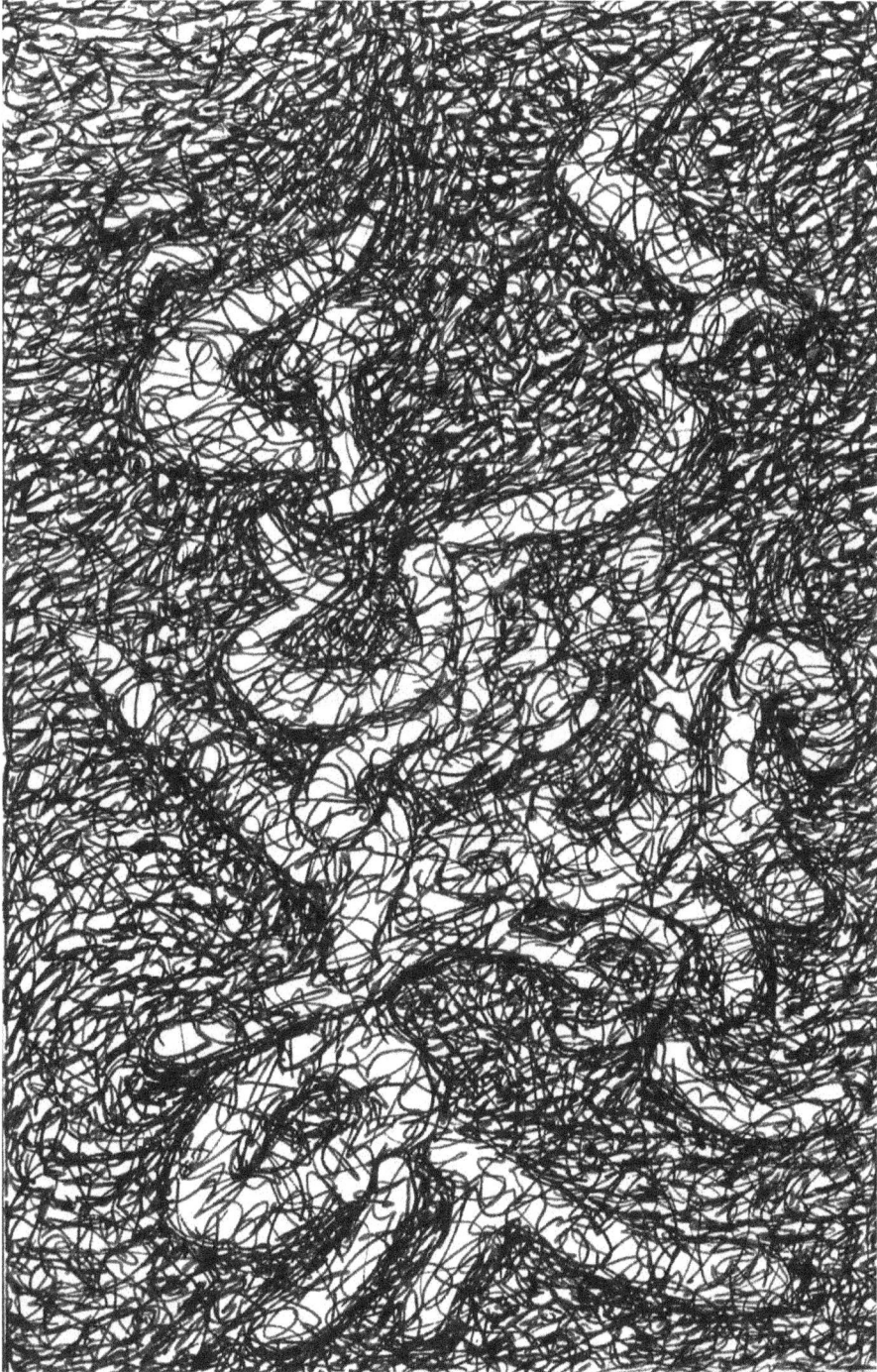

35

When certain Tuesdays are too agitated, or pass in too much of a hurry, the Curtain intervenes to temper them, or (where appropriate) to make them run more gently. That's the case, usually, of the Tuesday before the Awakening Wednesday, which is a Tuesday of top speeds. If not careful, you may start counting your bones on Monday evening and get to the second bone on Wednesday, because Tuesday passed by rushing, unheard, and took with it all intermediary bones between bone 1 and bone 2 (including the swimming tibia, that you wear only on Thursdays). The Curtain doesn't like those brisk evolutions, they appear vulgar to her and in disagreement with the general movement of time, which should be (she thinks) slow. In order to slow down the speed of a fast Tuesday, the Curtain attacks it simultaneously from three places (at dawn, after noon, and toward dusk), hitting it with a tenderness that diminishes its vigor. Dawn freezes between purple shrouds and an unsure azure, noon hours don't flow forward any more, toward the shore of the siesta, but spin in wide polar circles, and sunset falls flat in the arms of the new morning. On a wall, where Tuesday stopped its run, appears a concave X.

36

In the X zones of the Curtain, vocal speech is not used and the locals speak only through saps. At the moment of speaking (a special moment, announced by an emission of spores), one's sap gets into another one's stem, mixing with its sap and, thus, speaking what the speaker has to say. There are saps that don't say a big deal (only where something got broken again), but others bear important messages: *I, egg. You, fire.*

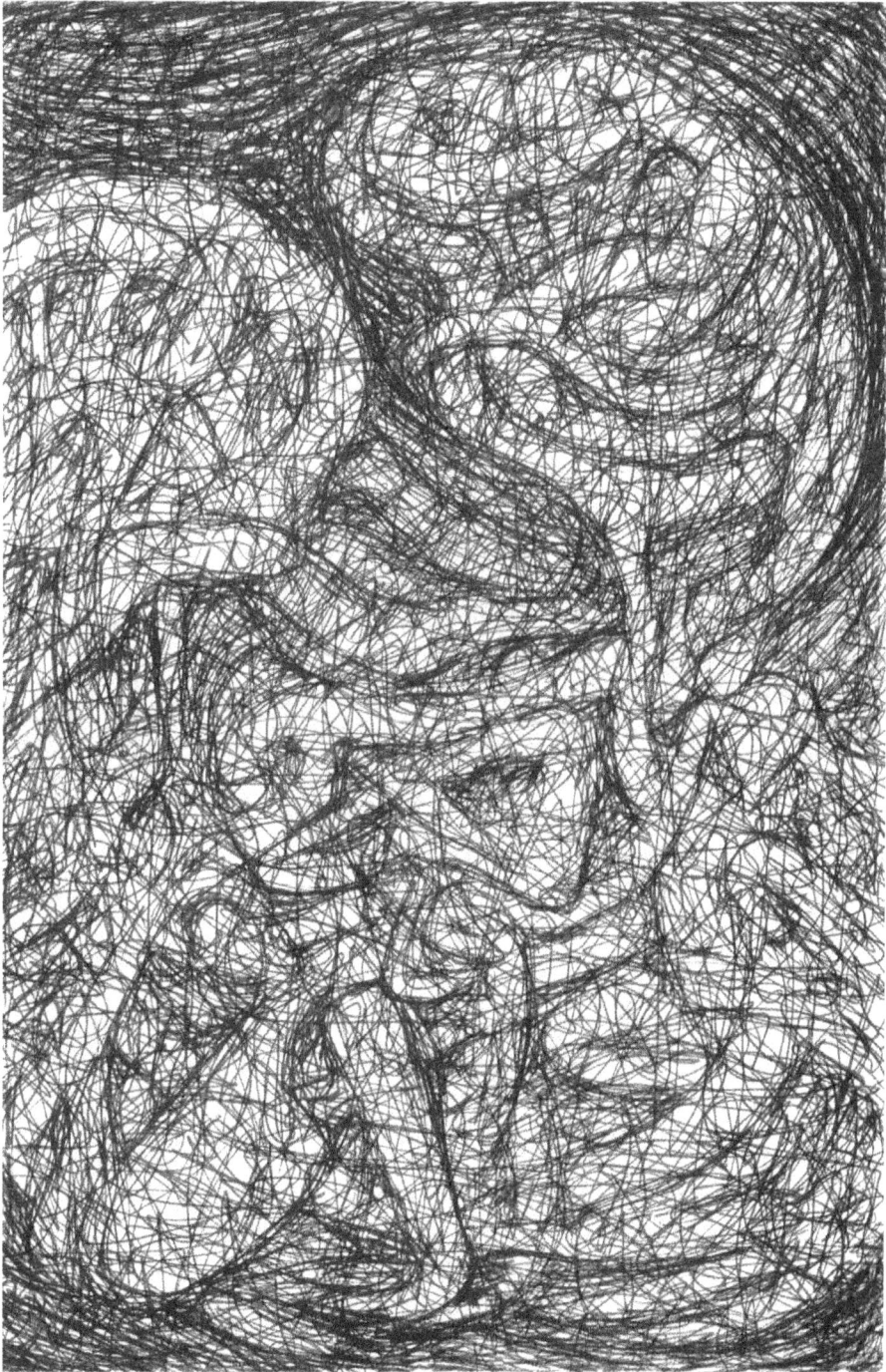

37

It's only natural that, under the rind of a sentence, there should be a core. Empty sentences, where the core hasn't curdled (such as "We used up our exaltation and tackled correctly complex aspects, but the landscape didn't answer in kind"), are rare. Even rarer are the sentences with two cores, which are joined by a ladder—you reach the second after you unveiled the first, but an unveiling can extend up to six years and many give up. They think that one core is enough, so why would they climb up to its pair? However, double cores (as speech athletes know so well) impart sentences a face.

38

Between the moment when a sentence dies away and the moment when another begins to breathe, on the voice's surface there appear shadows or vapors that remove the dust from it and smooth it out. The shadows remove the deposits of discursive dust with certain fingers specific to them, while vapors clear it by means of an electric counter-dust operated through mumbling. Then, the smoothing of the vocal sur-face (both by shadows and by vapors) is achieved with the help of an ample lantern consisting of three fascicles of warm smells woven into a single stream, that the shadows or the vapors move over the speaker's mouth. This intermezzo of oral terrain restoration is called the *Antroca Intermezzo* (or the *Antroca Interval*) after the name of the speaker in whose mouth it was first discovered and studied. In the case of tall speakers, but also of speakers with shorter bones talking from atop of a hill, there were registered, on an average, fifteen Antroca intervals in a discourse invoking draught, all of them followed by the drying of tree

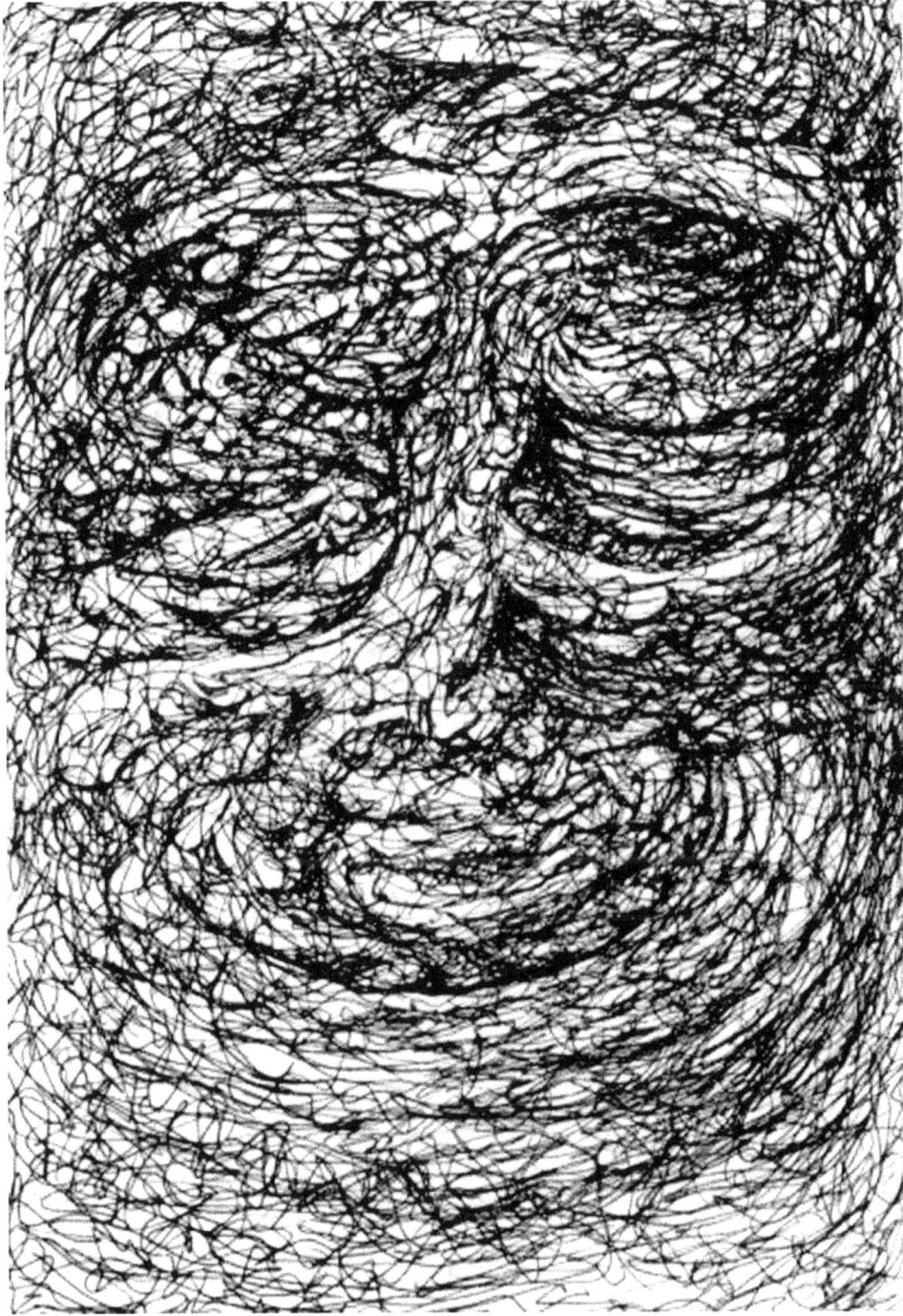

39

The Antroca Intervals appear not only between sentences, but also outside speech, on bodies. Between nose and pelvis, for example. Or between brow ridges and kneecaps. In the past, because of some shapes not cleared on time, the anatomy of the individual named Antroca underwent a permutation: he got a pelvic nose and a nasal pelvis, ocular kneecaps with mobile eyelids and eyebrows above the knees. In a few years, Antroca's whole anatomy got rearranged. His jaws became ankles and his ankles got teeth, his shoulders were replaced by buttocks, while his buttocks grew shoulder blades, his ears took the task of kidneys, and his kidneys could hear. Also, as a consequence of this string of mutations that destroyed him in order to rebuild his anatomy upside down, Antroca is now timeless. When intervals appear on his body (most often after he cries and tears gush out of his knees), those intervals have no duration—they have bulges.

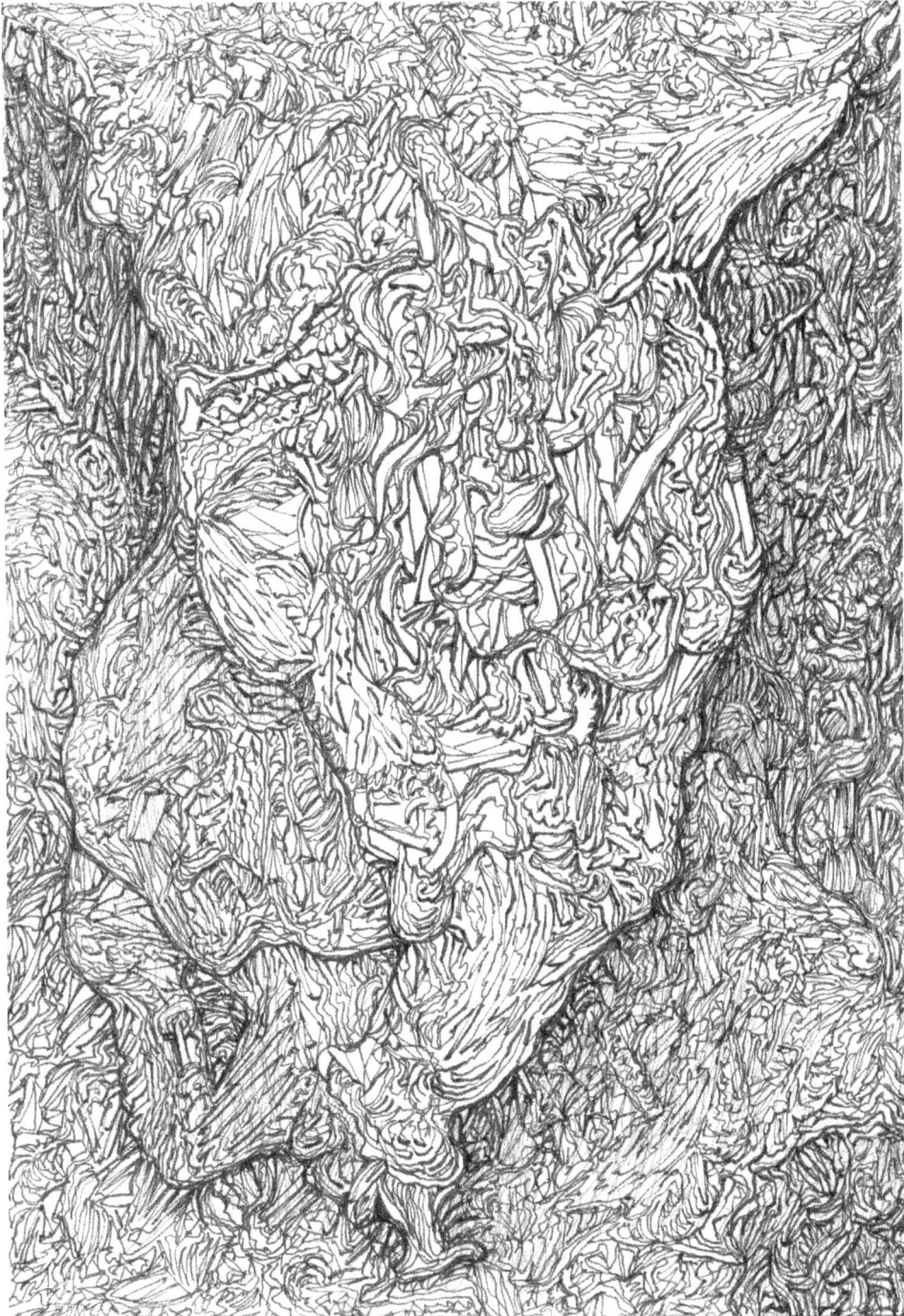

40

On simple bodies (such as the body of a medieval bicycle that didn't experience love first hand) the Antroca Interval bulges can be deceiving. Where there should be a fertile abyss with thousands of devices that recompose acoustically their mirrors, one sees a saline theater, an ensemble of grottoes lighted pecuniarilly. Instead of rivers, there are vertical canals, through which flows an infamous syrup, instead of beaches—pages from a contract. On the hills, 'dried up bogs are rising, while in the valleys (as days go by), the wind is laid down. Large surfaces of dust, threatened by frost, migrate toward a second, more western, South.

The glacial amphitheaters are not immense either. Some have their fangs retracted inward and erosion clothes them in caramel tones; above some other, cupolas—that break light, bringing it to the state of flake—have arched. It could appear, as it is seen on the go, an unfortunate landscape, residue of an extinction, were it not for the intervention of the three.

41

Miss Uno arrives the first, in a dress with teeth that will devour a slice from each and every thing (avoiding the things that are not sliceable, like art, but biting their nose upon seeing them). Behind her comes Mister Minus with his analysis rake, gathering the ambience in round heaps, in order to comment on it the next day with a cool head. (A commentary meant to be balanced on the East-West axis, and profound on the North-South axis, will always start with the breaking down of a theme in a series of assimilable elements, and the primordial element for a cool-headed commentator is the heap, because it has a high degree of assimilability). Mister Minus takes an aspect from heap A, peels it, and starts to chew on it. The aspect is sweet, therefore his commentary will be in an acid register. Now Miss Terminus shows up, emerging with difficulty from the geometry where she spent the night. She leaves behind her a trail of boiling coins—they are all 9-cent coins, with the exception of an 88-cent coin, which has the effigy of Reason on the obverse.

42

The contradictory image of Reason appears like a female Janus on the 88-cent coin's obverse. It has two profiles—one clear, the other one veiled. On its pate, in a closed vessel, two claws rip the uncertainty, to prove what it is not. On its forehead—clouds, from which come out animal arms. On its lips—a hatchet in mourning.

The 88-cent coin's reverse (which boils only at 0° and emits an elliptical vapor) bears the image of a raft, out at sea. It's a numismatic way of suggesting the movement of *this* Reason on a liquid route.

43

Oftentimes, on certain less circulated seas, one can see floating knots. Some of them are big, like the interval between 6AM and 10AM, others are tiny, like the size of a country. The waters' connoisseurs fear them because they are voracious, they gulp down almost anything and cannot be kept at a distance, no matter how skillful one's compass may be. Nordic blind people know how to avoid them.

These floating knots gather in families, in order to dominate more easily the surfaces they cover. Or in order to brave certain hostile apparitions: a swarm of labels, whose venom can take one apart instantaneously and break one's simplicity, an oceanic bull surging unexpectedly from behind a wave with a gaff between its horns and releasing love-squirts from its hooves, some semi-liquid lizards in search of a certain enzyme, or other anti-knot creatures. They cannot be vanquished on one's own, but only by getting multiplied.

A knot family has from a hundred to four thousand members, without counting misalliances, such as those between a premature knot and a noose. A less numerous family, like the screen-knot family (with only 388 members) needs for nourishment a whole nation of food daily.

This—but also more obscure causes, such as the double-dealing of calendar breeders—explains the galloping increase of edible nations.

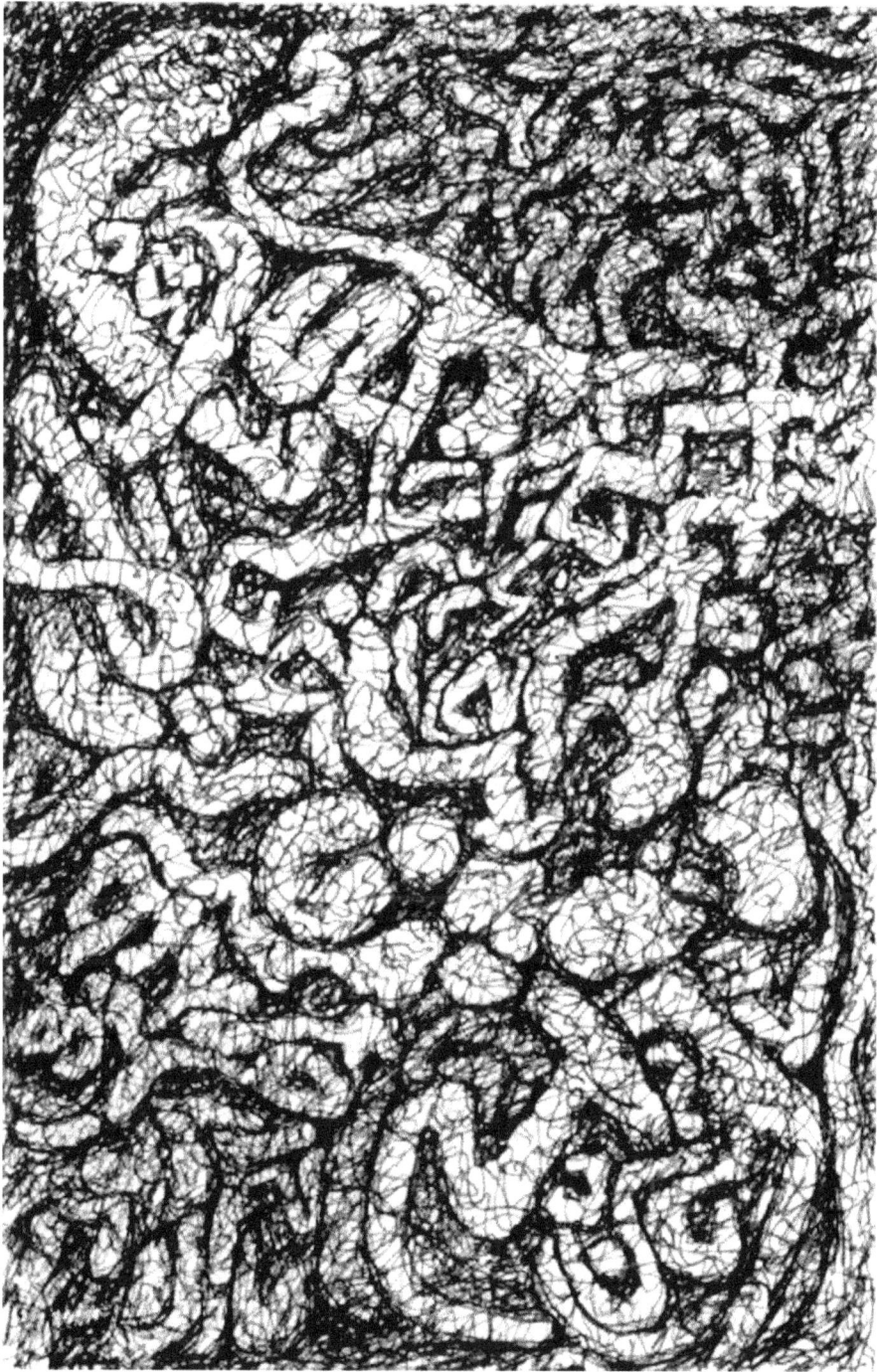

44

Screen-knots were—until they gathered in a family—plow-knots. They plowed. Not because they liked plowing, or wanted to organize their lives in agrarian cycles, but because a knot who is at his beginnings works his way only by plowing. For a young (even pubescent) knot, to plow is a formative labor, through which he reaches maturity and can integrate himself in the adults' fabric. Therefore, plowing age, in a knots' society, is the age when an ephebe loses his juvenility.

At night, when the day would diminish on walls and become opaque, they plowed the light. They plowed it deep, from the high plateaus toward the plains, with all their four tentacles, cleaving it, and not stopping when it moaned. Then, in the plowed light, which exuded summer vapors, they sowed oxygen grains. In the morning, when night emptied its arteries one by one, and its black blood diluted in the foam of dawn, they plowed the darkness. More tenderly this time, trying not to touch its labial nerves, which would have cramped. In the furrows they tossed lightning bolt seeds, voluble ones.

45

The lightning bolt seeds thrown by the plow-knots into the furrows of darkness keep on blabbering, without giving their mouths a rest. They wouldn't stop, or pause to listen to other spoken words. They don't have a silence organ like the rain seeds, who are quiet liquidly and talk only unheard, in between drops. For the lightning seeds, words are growth movements, and speaking is their manner of sprouting.

After three months of incessant talking, in chorus, germination draws to an end. From the seeds grow thin, but aggressive, lightning bolts, who pierce the film of darkness and fill the night field with ears. On top of each ear, a group of still soft polyhedrons, summary developed, starts pulsating—meekly at first, then vehemently. At that moment, the seeds say "Zero" (it's their last say) and retreat from creation.

Upon hearing "Zero" (which sounds like wheels grinding inside a ball), all ears erupt and send a gush of warm echoes ("Zeeee..." at 118°F, and "...errro" already boiling) toward the beardless polyhedrons. Presently, on the cheek of the central polyhedron appears the beard of a patriarch from Antioch, killed by impetigo while kneeling in front of the sea to ask for its mercy. On the faces of several side polyhedrons, from nothing-ness (albeit a hairy one), appear mustaches of Hispanic viceroys and, respectively, of sweet-mannered Taras Bulbas. The fringe polyhedrons get wavy Assyrian beards, through which run microbes of astral origin, consuming the matter of memory in their race. And so on, and so forth, until, weighed down by the burden of those exuberant facial append-ages, polyhedrons break up and fall down.

46

Falling polyhedrons don't have arms. They only have a short inferior member (in the shape of a retracting needle, which serves as a call receptor) and four internal members, located in the stomach, to digest movement. They are dynamic bodies, often with several independent existences, but which can sometimes collide. At a certain level of splendor, when polyhedrons have accelerated their fall through a contraction, those separate existences end up overlapping.

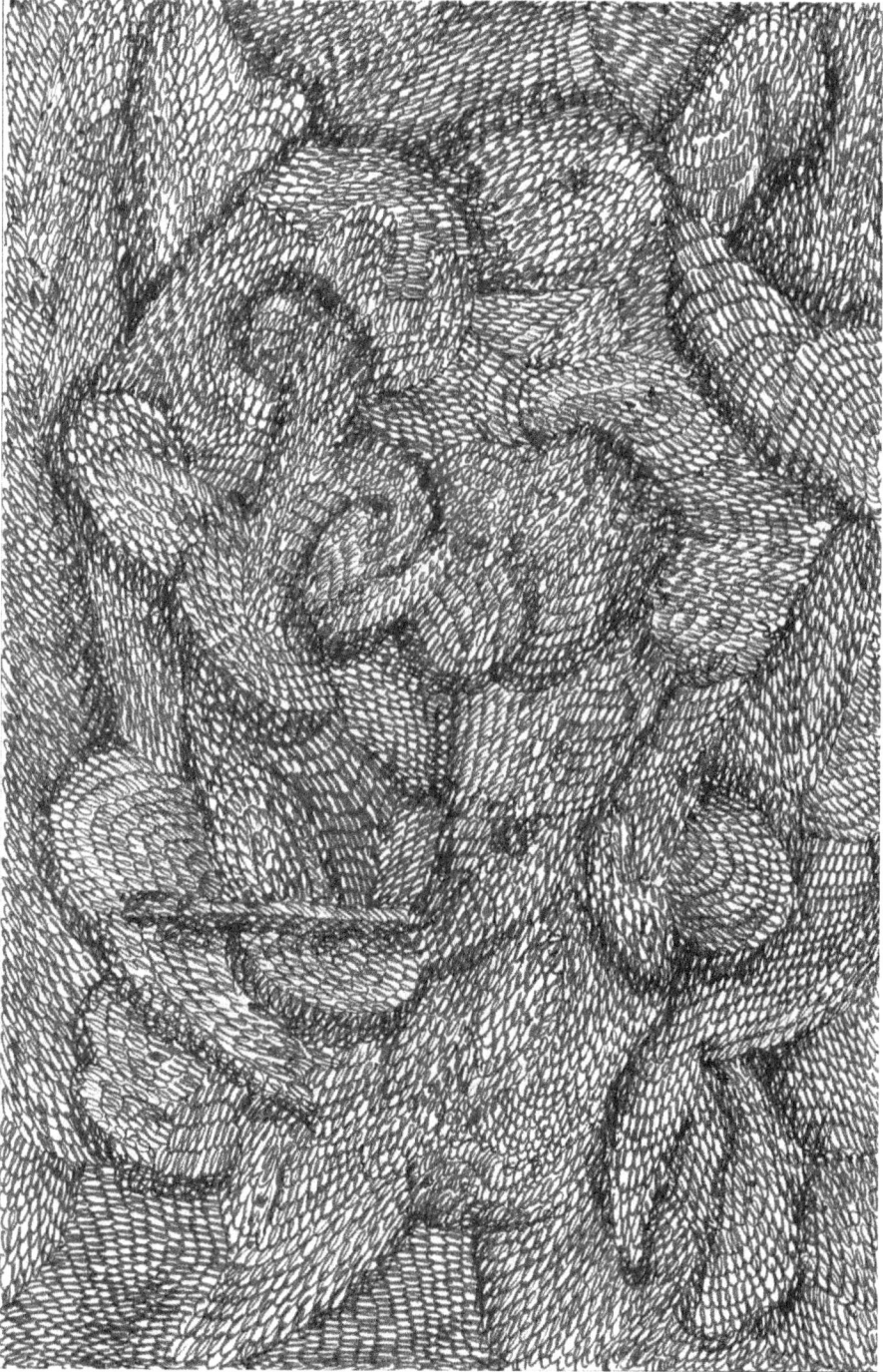

47

An unending row of windows, and beyond them, in an external sitting room without walls and with a transparent ceiling, two immense circles that overlapped. Before overlapping, the first circle was red and the second yellow. However, their overlapping didn't result in an orange circle, but in a white one. On this white circle flows a vertical river, its waters golden on the surface and black in the depths—it's a kind of theoretical Nile, or (for the fans of Egyptian geometry) an adaptation of the idea of Nile to the idea of circle. Which circle has five centers, all in the South.

In the first center, a fellah is irrigated by the stars. Several constellations (of which we can mention the Occipital Rein Constellation and the Thesis Constellation) have dug irrigation canals in his body and are sending fluids through them to fertilize him. The fellah seems ready to reach the *moist* stage, because his voice got green and he started to mutter the germination mantra.

In the second center (identical to the first, but with other aromas), an inflatable Ramesses fills up his temple with a typhoon in order to depopulate it. He doesn't want to be adored by his people any more, he doesn't want more flowers and oils, more symmetrical offerings at each equinox and eructation. He would like to spend the next hundred years on a rug of insults.

In the third center (marked Beta) there is a pharaoh too, but a Nordic one, donning a navy blue alpaca costume with lightning bolts on its lapels. He caresses the skin of a soup forbidden to commoners, giving himself to sadness.

The fourth center is empty, and in the fifth nightfall came.

48

Between those centers go—on ropes—the gods of the circle to inspect the situations and then to decide what to do with them. Some situations can fill a box (that one can keep, or not); others can be woven into weapons and tools.

The situational revolver is such a weapon. Woven from three related situations (one of mental partition, one of solving the nation traumas, and one of loss), said revolver kills acid rains that may still fall unjustly, and it has the function of a chronometer, measuring accurately an ecstasy's duration at noon.

Among the tools, the rake and the wheelbarrow, both woven from moribund situations, have the most work to do: the gods use them to bundle rebel fibers into one single void.

49

For the subgods, finding a box with situations tossed on a heap of divine trash is a triumph. "There," they say to themselves, "today the trash is rich." They dance happily around it, tumble, and clap their hands to show their joy at the surprises of squalor. Then, they open the box carefully, so as not to frighten some of the situations, or spill their aromas. In the box, set in rows of four, the situations sleep. (It's a dynamic sleep, in which turquoise and crab can unite on a reciprocal bed sheet.) Each second situation dreams something identical (for example, a lumbar tree grown from an emotion), and from those pairs of dreams flow rabbits.

(The rabbits' colors alternate: one black rabbit, two white, one red, one white rabbit, two red, one black, one red rabbit, two black, one white, and so on. In a white rabbit can fit about forty not too tall guards, their legs torn out, and the quantity of apodal guards per square rabbit is measured in mysteries, or, if necessary, in liters per smoke. In a red rabbit fits a quarter of the railway-elephant's intelligence, after said elephant had his hat taken out of his abdomen and was bathed in coals. In a black rabbit fits only fifteen drawer-jellyfish maximum, who have lived the illusion experience to the fullest.)

For a while, the subgods stay bent over the situations, watching their sleep, and absorb their double dreams with a straw. When they are filled up and cannot absorb any more, they stop watching. A more daring subgod takes a situation (or a series of situations) out of the box, and signals the four experts to approach.

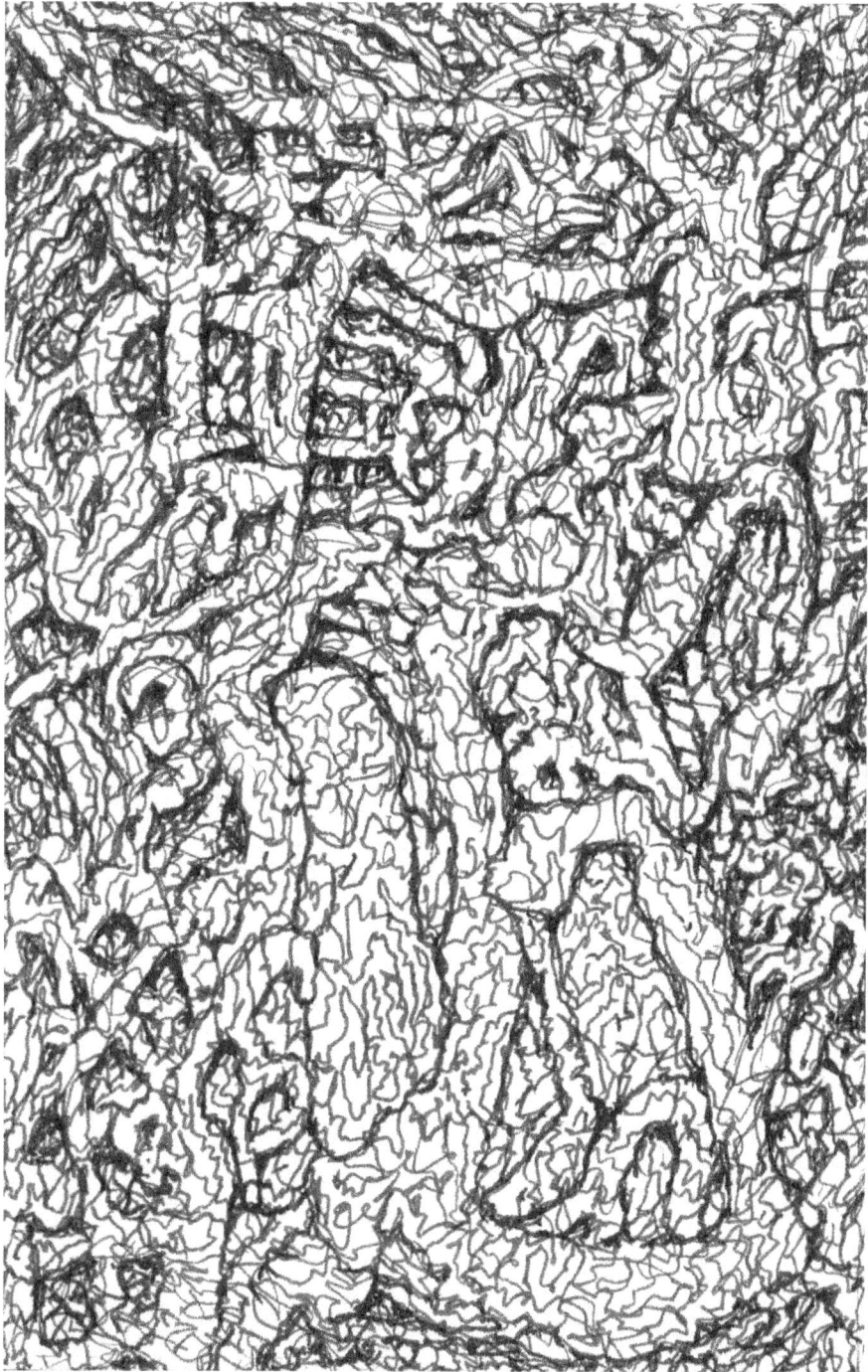

50

First appears the Ascertainer. His job is to ascertain, as precisely as possible, the situation. He is a black individual, no taller than a cane and completely blind. In order to ascertain, he introduces an arm into the situation, pulls some strings, and searches (gropingly) for one of their ends. Having found it, he smells it with a finger, then sucks it with the same finger to find out what's wrong. After the Ascertainer comes the Isolator—he is stately, ruddy, with unprecise gestures, but with a jeweller's precision in his hints. He isolates thermally the situation zone by covering it with a veil of spittle. Now it's the Separator's turn to spring into action. This one, even if he lost his human form, doesn't seem to be an alien, because he is clothed in stones. In order to be an efficient separator, one needs a lot of free space, that is obtained by cheering (which, the same as idleness, has a devastating effect on crowded spaces), and has to know well where the limits are fragile. The Separator, after he emptied the space with an explosion of yodels, hits the situation limit between the second and third vertebrae, thus separating it from the neighboring situations. (Through separation, a situation blooms.) Then intervenes the last expert, the Consumer (a veteran of static riots), who takes the situation and drinks it.

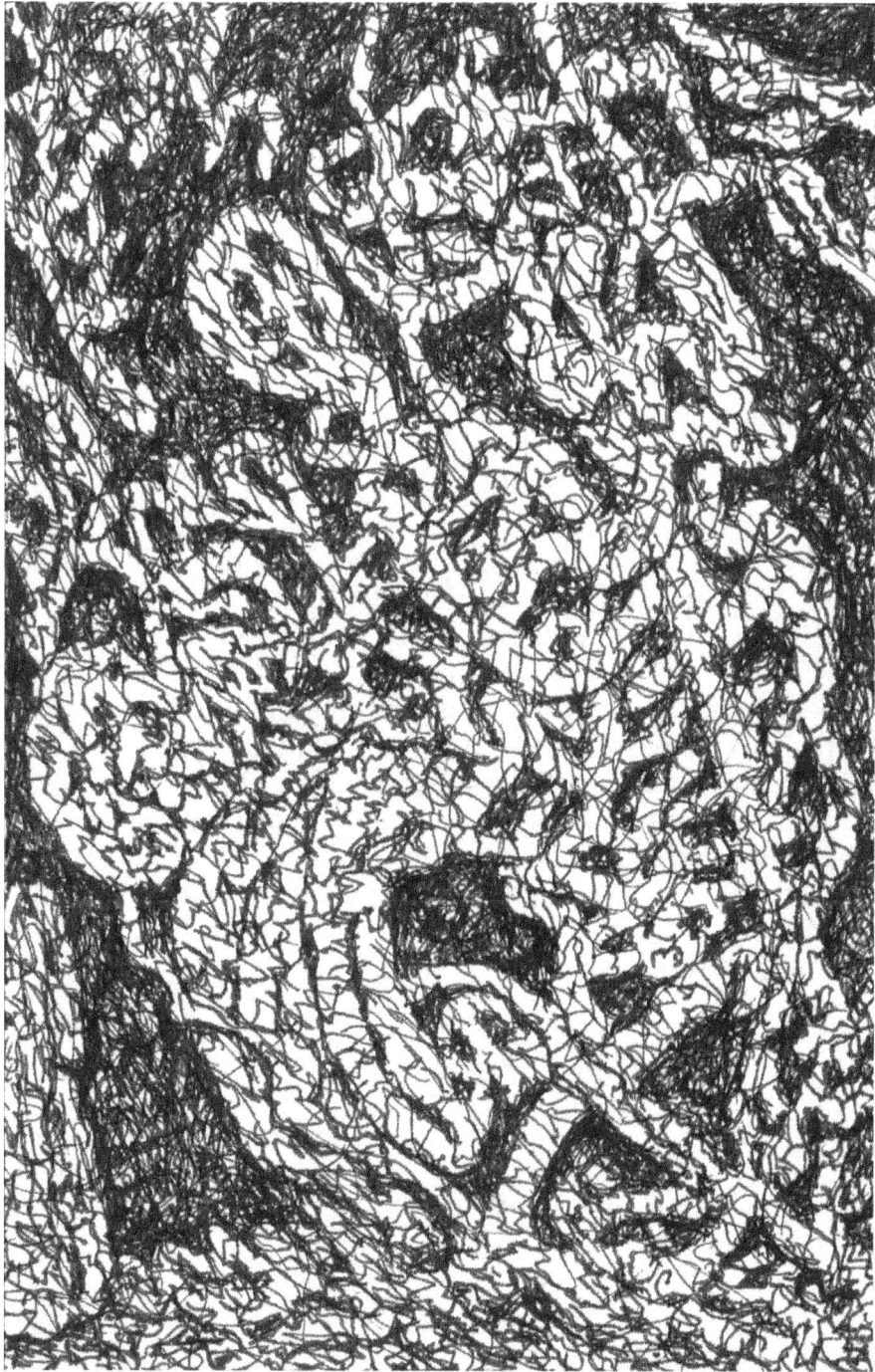

51

The first dissolving (of a black vapor in a metal) has at both ends an emulsion and a powder. The emulsion and the powder will turn sour through cold baking, but without their opposite jellyfish being separated—they are sewn together. Being sewn, they will become the rain's pillow. The second dissolving (of four centuries of red in the sleeping rain) does not start until the brachial oil will boil, the arms of the young shade being stretched out. Because of the shade pushing the vault and slowing it somewhat, the air becomes matte. The third dissolving (of the slow wheel in itself) attracts the obscure elements into a separation: the iron with flesh cheeks is diverted toward milk, the senile oxygen hides itself in screams ("Vulf, vulf!" it will scream from there, to cover its presence), the attacking clay loses its fingernails one by one, it's decaying until its clouds burn out—and it's gone.

These three dissolvings, equal in duration, through which the dynamic space will be emptied of vibrations, will be followed by a series of eight optical duels between pairs of sounds.

52

In the work of a qualified Consumer, there appear sometimes tough situations that he cannot drink. (Compared to those, the optical duels between pairs of sounds are a trifle.) Among such situations there is the one called "Moto & Mummies," in which a non-existent dog named Moto is attacked by a large group of mummies with the intent of making it exist. For a Consumer, this is a situation with a high level of difficulty of the type either/or. Either Moto will end up existing and will be devoured by the mummies, or the mummies will hit the wall of the dog's non-existence and die of sorrow. In order to solve conveniently this situation and satisfy both parties, the Consumer spreads a canvas over it. The canvas hides perfectly the whole situation, and Moto & Mummies are left to their own devices.

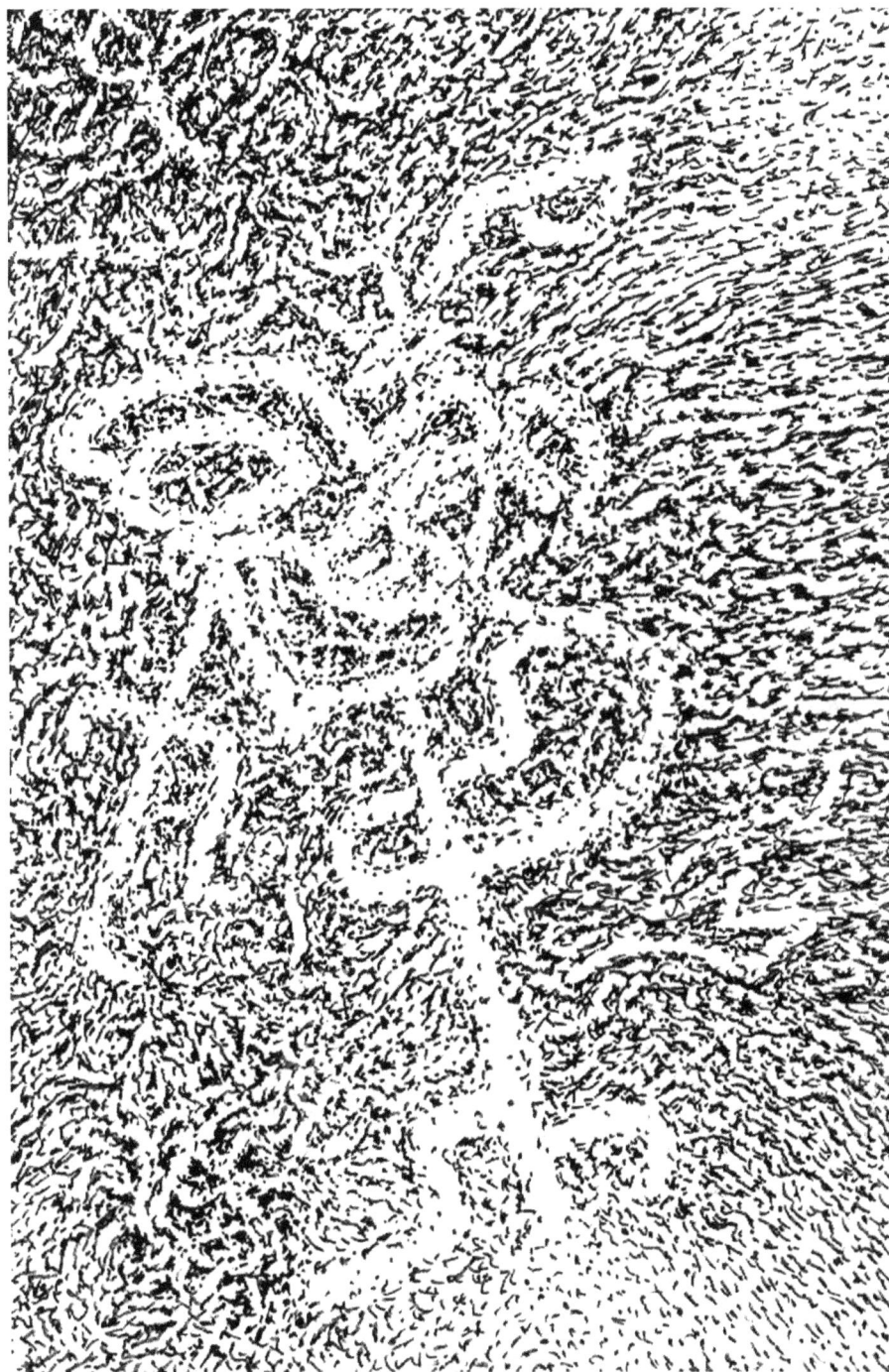

Non-ones are not different from non-others just because they share the same *non*. Convergent disjunctions are familiar to both the one and the other. When you ask a non-one about the weather, a non-other will answer that it's sunny in flurries.

A negative individual passing in front of a greedy theory was put (by the passing itself, because passing is a calling) in the situation of choosing between taking off his shoes mentally, or disappearing. In order not to disappear (it was rather early for that), he took his shoes off his head, and took to classifying the situations into three large groups. The first group consists of *simple situations with a single drawer*, the most common example of such situation is when someone wakes up above oneself, after having gone to sleep within oneself the previous evening. The second group comprises *replacement situations* (they are about three thousand, if we also count the perturbed replacement situations). In a replacement situation, the same someone (or someone else) has to build a cold identity out of clay and a few rods. (Or out of warm air and feathers, or out of dried fruit that one lines up on a string, or out of oil and smoke, or out of remains of decomposed organisms, etc.). In the third group we find the dead end situations, named *double advantage situations*, when the non-ones come, and the non-others leave.

55

A double advantage situation is that of an empty place after the non-others left, and the non-ones came. The non-others' departure emptied the place, but the non-ones' arrival didn't fill it, because the non-ones are rare. In such a situation, the place has nothing else to do but fill itself with Quarters and Halves, who will fight each other (with domestic weapons) to transform the place into an anti-place.

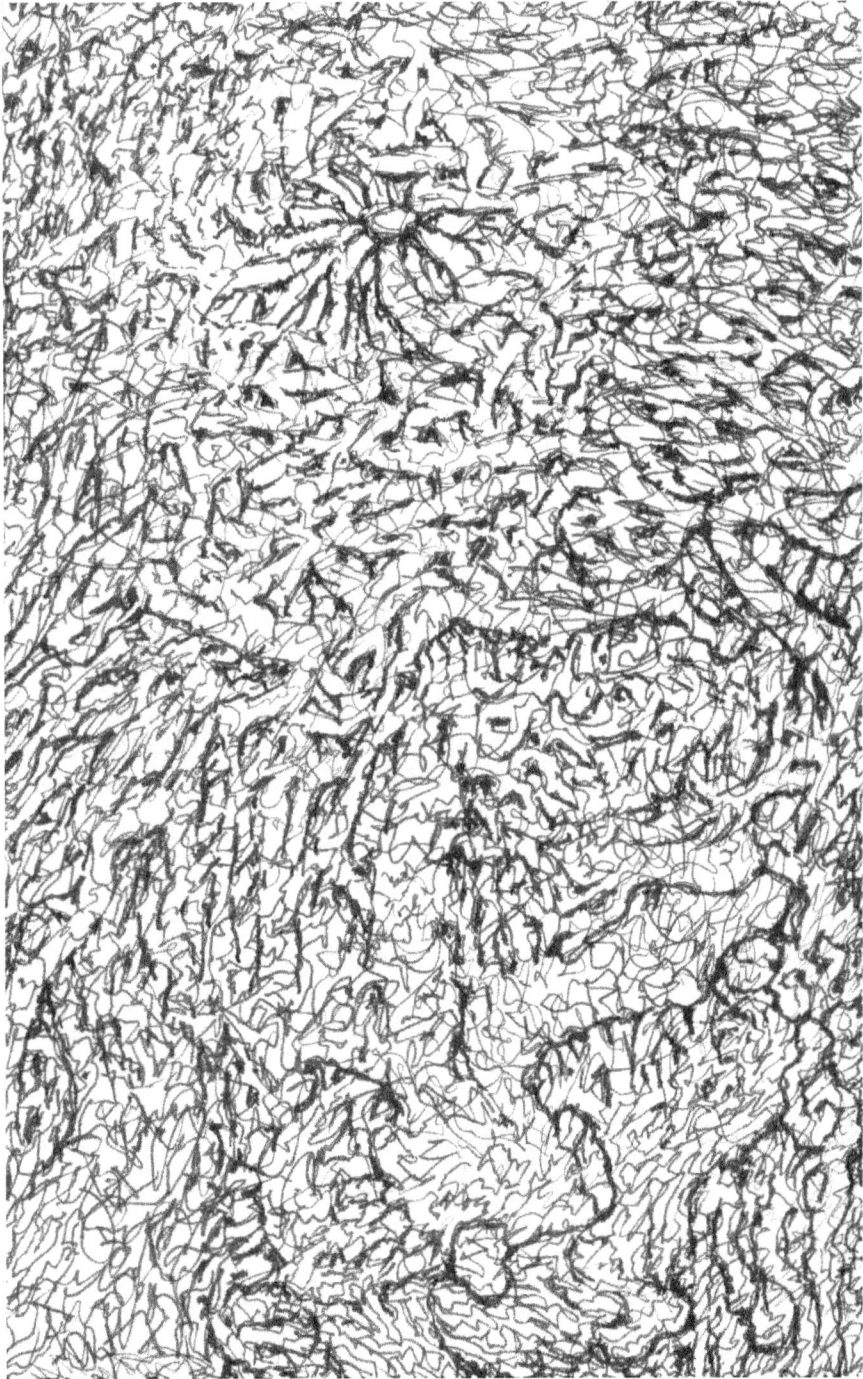

56

The battle between Quarters and Halves, which took place near the only active carnivorous spoon, started with a rain of seeds, and ended, three days later, with the fall of a chair from the sky. Between those two moments, the Quarters lost half of their bodies, and the Halves were left without a quarter of their suction cups. The initial moment (the rain of seeds) was accompanied by a rise of the horizontal temperature on the coast and by the blocking of the vertical temperature between the *grave* and *acute* levels. (In tombs, the recent dead woke up bewildered, wondering where to go. "Go behind the century," an older dead told them, who was turned face down to whiten. To which, they started to hop, out of joy, like pieces of wood in a clubhouse.) After that, the temperatures melted into each other, forming a stable cyclone fluted in places, which gave the occasion to the Quarters to roll in embers (to refresh their incandescence), and to the Halves, to sharpen their gaze with a flux of ointments. The final moment (the fall of the chair from the sky) was perceived differently by the two camps, by now in the third day of fighting, when they were all thinking of peace. For the Quarters, the chair was a manifestation of the divine will, its fall meaning the return to origins. For the Halves, a chair (no matter how it looked and where it fell from) was nothing but a chair to sit on and wait.

57

The second part of the drama unfolds in the region of the "tubes." (It was preceded by a few skirmishes between armies of eagles with W-shaped spurs, a dagger exchange under the window of too full a heart, and the short flight of the underground aviator above the Great Field.) The Queen (a rotation) and the King (a mechanism), both dead, bent over the world to look for their babe in an old star. Animals in mourning, their fur covered by the snow of the latest scorching heat, graze some strings somewhere. From their hooves grow sickles, from their horns grow ladders. Water climbs up on one of them, but it doesn't reach the top (where it would calm down); it remains a wave. A "tube" sips it.

58

One of the forgivable errors that a "tube" can commit—only when it has no choice—is placing a muscular W on an M surface. (M surfaces are those musical surfaces where music resounds matte, and the sounds, when lacking brightness, are perceived as nuances of certain smells.) On such a surface there can be placed, at random, or in an order dictated by the preferences of the "tube" for one voice or another, different melodic structures, starting with the vocal lint in cascade, and ending with the vibration scale of a caravan stopped at a traffic light, but it is recommended that muscles be absent from the composition of such structures, because a muscle (be it even atrophied, or flabby) produces unwanted contractions of the M surface. Such a contraction of the M surface means, for a "tube," the end.

However, there appear situations when the "tube" is obligated (by its own tubularity) to make a decision at the cost of its life and to place a muscular W on an M surface, at the edge.

59

Now, from the muscular W placed on the M surface, the bride is born. It's a birth in colored pains, from the top down, from forehead toward embankment. First, the reflexion muscle appears, which is an introductory muscle, having the shape of a thinking mouth. It will present to the green audience, in simple three-syllable words ("o-ga-ne", "tel-la-yi", "ter-nu-vo," and others), the bride's architecture, so that the audience can discuss it. The discussions can last for several days, during which there appear (placing themselves where they belong) the education, death, and numerator muscles, each one of them accompanied by its own skin. (Subsequently, those isolated fragments will entwine, forming a whole: the bride's night epidermis.)

After the discussions' conclusion, and after taking note of the audience's suggestions, the marital mechanism that produces the bride interrupts its working for a few minutes to change what needs to be changed, then resumes it. There appear the simplicity muscle (red on the exterior, with crystalline striations), the twin muscles that help the jaw slide on an inclined plane, the muscle of habit (wrapped on an axis with a double metronome), a muscle for maintaining fright, and two random muscles, whose functions are obscure.

At this stage, the bride is only lacking, in order to be muscularly complete, the absence muscle, and a pair of lacrimal muscles. They appear, splitting the heavy air, out of a question.

60

A valley. In the valley, a river (a single one, equal to itself). In the river, the bride (floating). The bride's floating has three reference moments: 1) ante-now floating; 2) now floating; 3) post-now floating. In the reference moment 2 ("now floating"), which is a compact moment, as opposed to moments 1 and 3, which are less dense, the bride floats face down, analyzing a cavity, namely the Perlo cavity of the wedding.

Here is the definition of the Perlo cavity in an *I Flow* dictionary: "A Perlo cavity is the spatial equivalent (often inaccurate from a metric point of view, but always sincere) of a postponement."

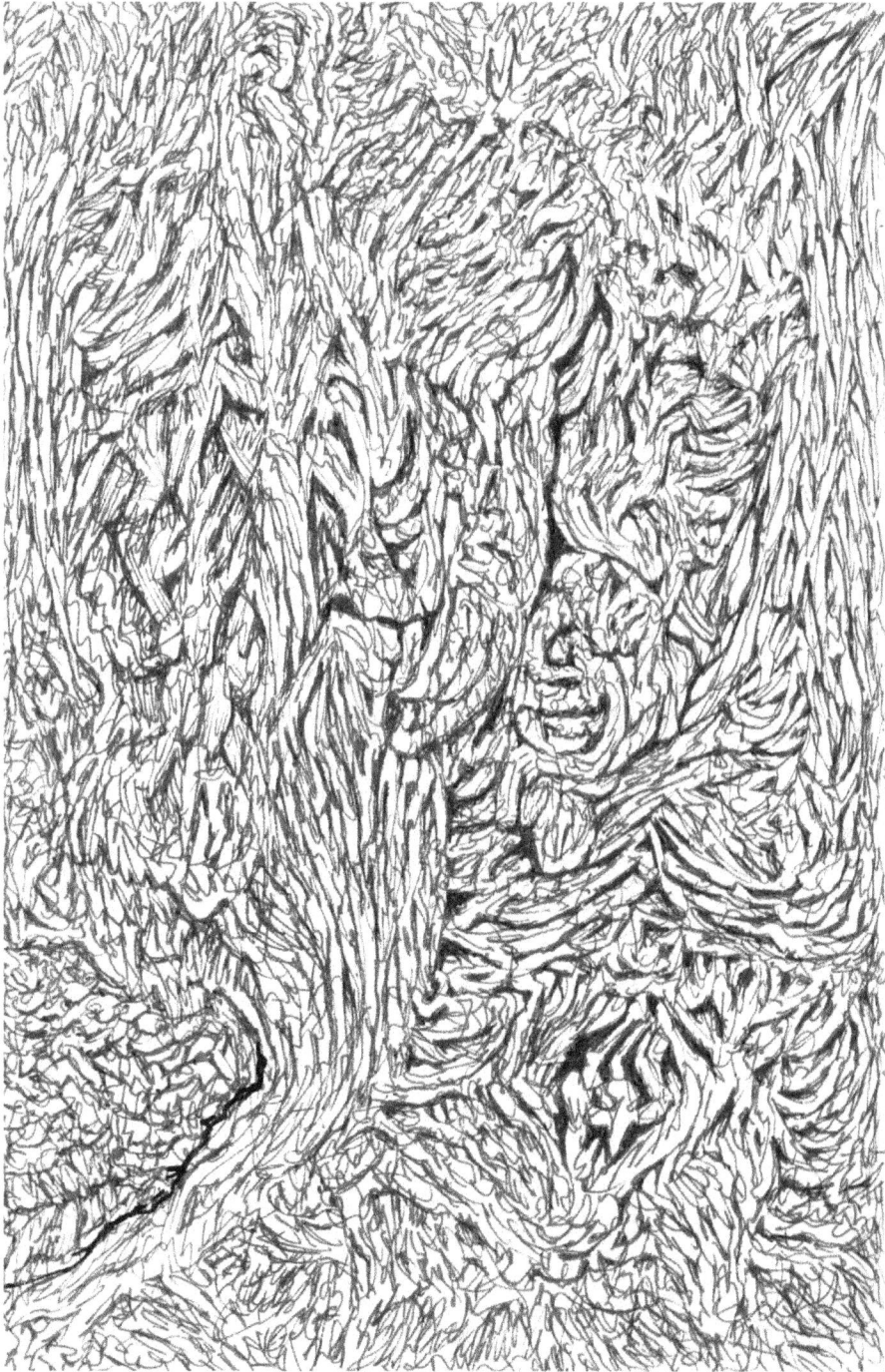

61

In the *I Flow* dictionaries used by rivers to disseminate their liquid information, or to dissolve the knowledge sediments that stand in their way, definitions are not immutable. A definition flows continually, and, by flowing, it compresses or swells, narrows or widens. If a statement is concise upstream (as in the definition of the egg: "The egg is an axis"), downstream it can acquire incantation inflexions ("Oh, you egg with steel arms, pillar of all creation!"), it can deteriorate in favor of an ampler explanation ("An egg—be it Egg One, or a regular egg—will not be easily awarded the rank of oval axis, but will obtain it only through striving and effort, laying itself continually"), or it can turn upside down (see the definition of axis omelette). Conversely, if upstream it was a fog-definition with obscure references (as in the definition of the monkey: "It is called *monkey* a metallic mesh, whose flaps kill bananas"), downstream it could become clear ("On the contrary, bananas have mouths").

By defining the world, with its forever unknown grottos and stretches of land, the rivers remake it.

62

Remaking the world, by defining it, is the work of four major rivers. Among those, only one (the Fructus Citronil River) can remake integrally the center of the world; the other three (the Bogha, Eleunethe and Yam-zo Rivers) remake only its shell, in places, where it's cracked.

Twice a year, in mid-April and in August, the waters of the Fructus Citronil River freeze, in order to gather strength. During those periods, the world-remaking activity is discontinued, the destruction agents can rise from silt and spring into action, and definitions are abandoned in the field, or tied up to a tree, as not to bite. The chair doesn't sing on roofs any more; in hearths, the viper ceases to burn. In grottoes, the trash collectors undulate and all is peaceful. The world opens up its core, which is devastated methodically by some white ants, with their fingernails.

63

From the valley (every world has a valley and a hill, even the vitrified ones), as one looks northward, where the clouds are burning, one sees the four sources of the Fructus Citronil River. One cannot see the first source very well, it's hidden in a limestone glove, over which some deafening reminiscences were deposited. The second one, on the contrary, is clear as mist: from the ear of a collapsed bishop there appears a torrent of green honey that cuts across his chest, flows down foaming toward the pelvic pulpit (where it is thickened by the tears of some nuns turned into stone) and, when nearing the ankles, it becomes tempestuous. The third source is subterranean, one can see only its neck covered with liquid scales and its central shoulders. (The nine lateral shoulders, that it shrugs when it is astonished, rest under a mountain of unconcern and rattle. With time, from rattling to rattling, from cracking noises of diluted bones and ripples of clavicles, a melody of dampness is taking shape.) The fourth source, being the essential one (because it contains in its waters the whole nucleus of the river), is farther away, on a stretch of nothingness.

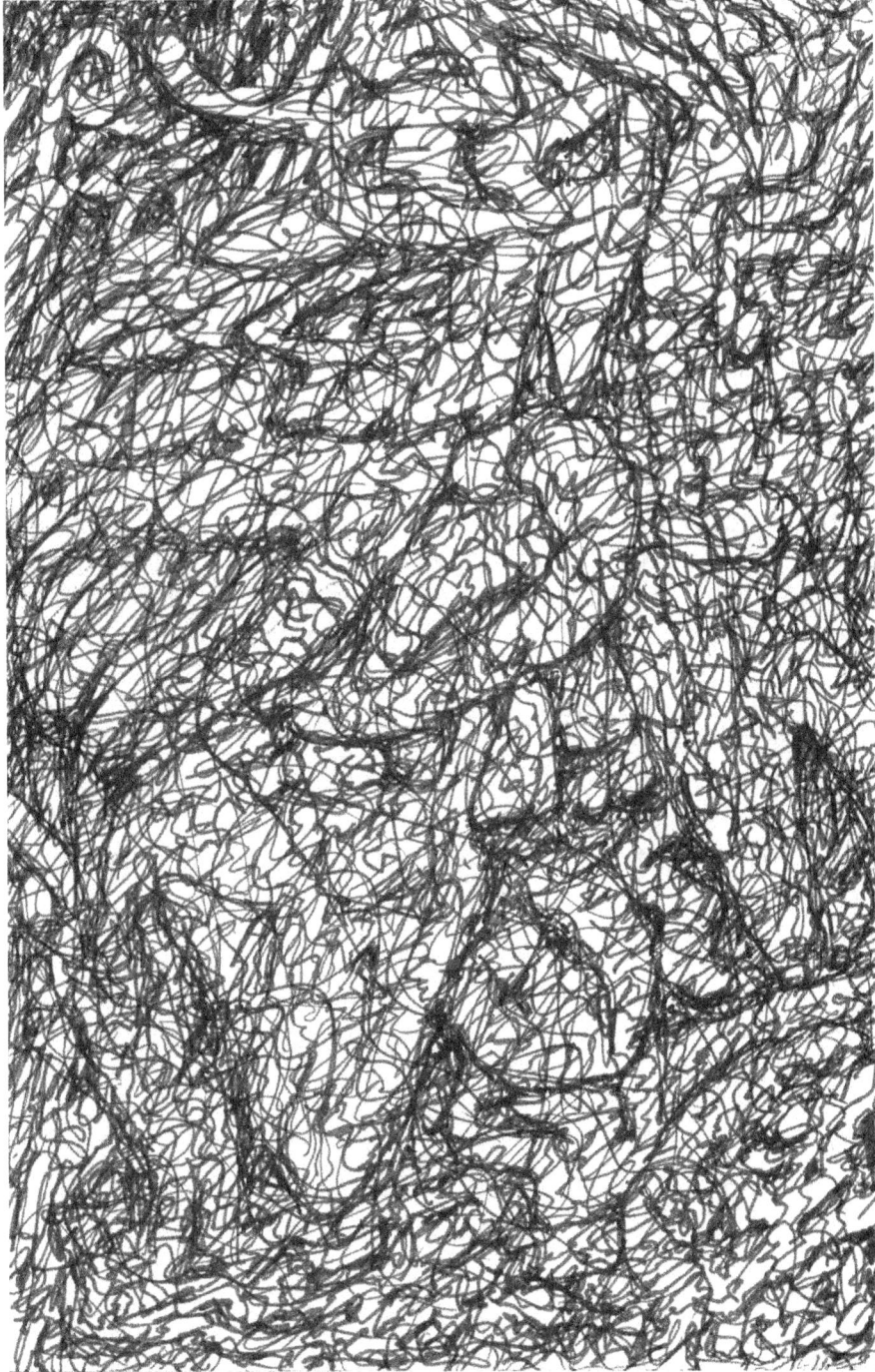

64

Nothingness or vice versa (some thing, that is), near the source, the bride is becoming round. Not because she would be the sum of all roundness (far from it—she is rather a tunnel with three ends), but her apparition has something to do with the genesis of a sphere. It's simple: when one says sphere, one means bride.

In a distance, nothing else comes even close to the form of a sphere (only sometimes, at enormous intervals, some needle). Therefore, for an onlooker not familiar with the marriage mechanism, the bride is a globe; or a balloon (for a sleeping onlooker, whose sight is divided in meta-sights, and has the tendency to snow lightly).

The complete bride, with an automatically cold complexion and her reduction area in expansion, sees her shield afire.

65

The most recent *I Flow* dictionary (the edition, from 2002, with drawers) defines a *menomenon* as the identical opposite of a phenomenon. Or— using the expression of a rural lexicographer, who is more interested in the words' speed, than in their adequacy to goals—as a "divergent twin." Furthermore, the example used by the dictionary's authors to illustrate the definition of the menomenon is the case of the inflamed bride, whose shield caught on fire.

"The bride with her shield aflame, who appears at the border between nothingness and accident," the dictionary says, "is a ferocious menomenon."

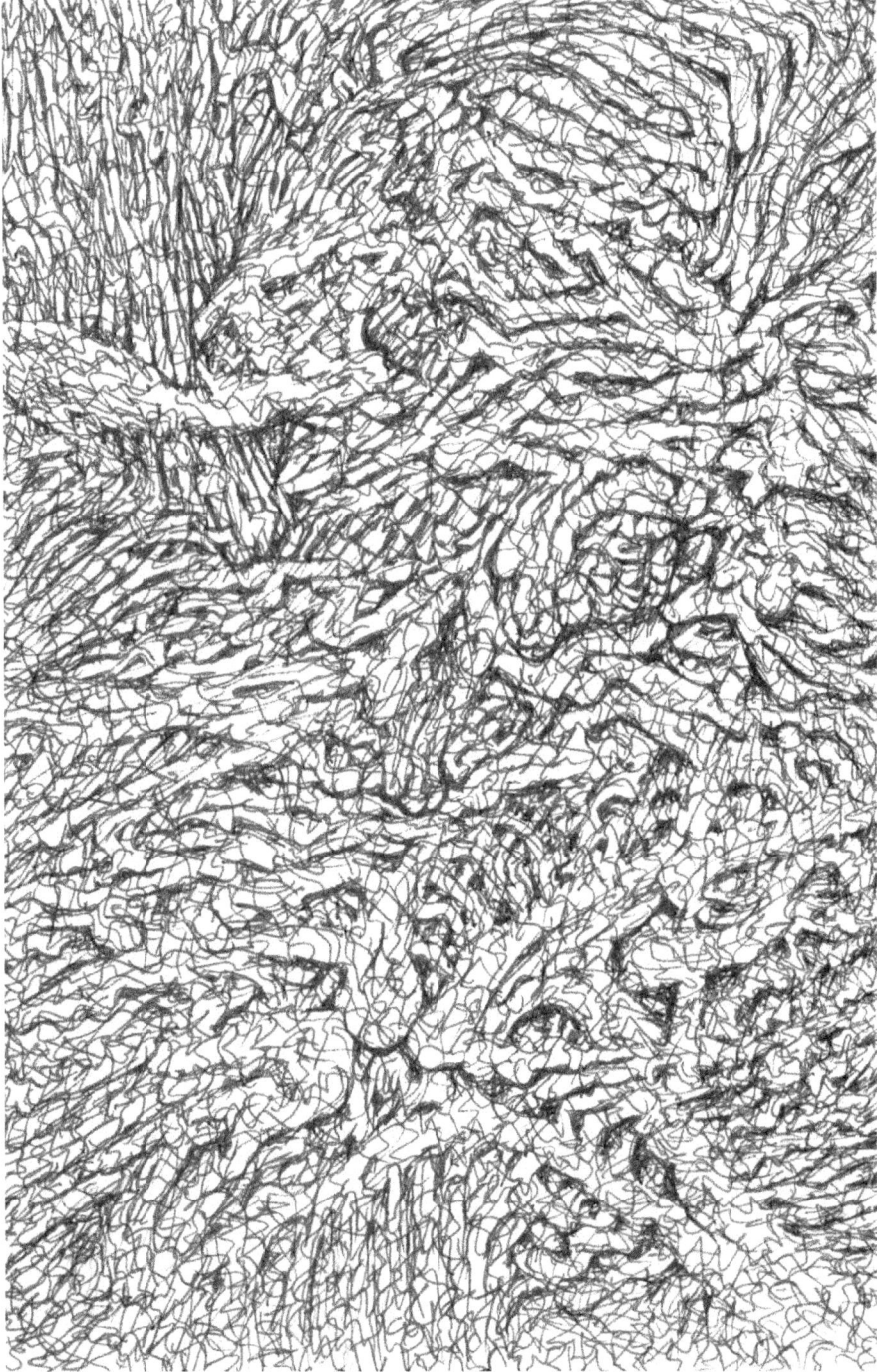

Being liquid

What is lies in what is not –Laozi

"The purpose of my automatic drawings is to explore what my unconscious can bring forth," Sasha Vlad says in an interview about his creativity. This time, he is not alone in doing that. Dan Stanciu explores such visions as well, but in writing. The *Sliding Ruins* book, which came about through the conjunction of images and words, is the objectification of a lucky constellation favorable to surrealist freedoms, consisting in *creative sharing*. It proves that from any image there can arise a story: suffice it to confer verbal power to it. When drawing, Sasha Vlad proceeds from concentrating on the automatic free flow of unsuspected stimuli, while Dan Stanciu observes the completed image in a kind of creative hypnosis, allowing enigmatic and explosive messages to speak by themselves. The inspiration for the stories to the given drawings works like an alpinist's hook in a rock: where there was nothing but vertical wall, a simple concentration creates a firm foothold for the safe ascent to the realm of spontaneous imagination.

The peerless style of Dan Stanciu's stories comes from his innate sense of ironic detachment. The composition of those drawn jungles transmutes for him into odd instructional texts. They resemble alchemical recipes for the fabrication of a *fool's stone*, even though they are written in the parlance of 21st century laboratories. For example, the author introduces to the inquiring reader the newly discovered *Gojo particles*, which "have a ceremonious-aberrant behavior and become luminescent when in contact with vinegar," or "spherical hay so indifferent, that its light absorbs any rustle." Ultimate arbitrariness is expressed here with scientific precision. In the course of this strange research process there is, for example, described an agent who "...even if he lost his human form, doesn't seem to be an alien, because he is clothed n stones." With the seriousness of a specialist's jargon there are delivered statements that are at the edge between a kind of physical philosophy and bound-less outrage: "Being liquid, for someone from the South, is a duty and a creed." It gets to unpredictable flashovers, where not a single sentence remains intact from the viewpoint of a limited mind: "In the Plantagenet branch, certain stars have golden collars to strangle His Highness with, when he overflows." In the middle of any such communication, the reader is left with completely no idea about which way it could conti-nue. Actually, it is precisely here that the intensity of those *dispatches from elsewhere* is grounded: the fact that they are able to constantly amaze, while they appear, from the beginning until the end, as though nothing has happened. It is clearly evident that the author doesn't in any way endeavor "to be humorous," but rather monitors the intrusion of unexpected jokes as a kind of intervention from outside, like, for example, during an intricate clarifying of a rather shady investigation of a "situation," which is handled in turn by several experts, each one of them having a specific function and ability—until, all of a sudden, "intervenes the last expert (...), who takes the situation and drinks it." The basic attribute of Dan Stanciu's texts is, however, something else than just humor. These are not just amusing stories and occasional anecdotes. Evidently, there is present a spontaneous and, therefore, poetically powerful *blending* of laughter and astonishment: in a joke there is a hidden confession—and vice versa. "By not flowing, one densifies and disappears," as, for instance, we can hear in an oracular incantation, which, in spite of its evident jocular character, unexpect-edly breaches into the realm of lyricism; the same as the sentence which looks as though it fell into the middle of scientist monologue directly from heaven: "The complete bride (...) sees her shield afire."

Also, for Sasha Vlad, every creative act begins by rejecting the illusion of the genius of his own intentions. "If my mind," he says, "is empty of any preconceived idea of what the drawing might be, then I'm ready." Even during the drawing process, the author gently monitors his hand to make sure it is not lead by any artistic "learned" movements, which would necessarily result in repeating what is already drawn: here, as well, any preconception is thus excluded from the completion of the work. Actually, the creative experience (not as some doctrine, but precisely as the only *experience* associated with *intuition*) guides Sasha Vlad, as well as Dan Stanciu and other surrealists, to the understanding of a seemingly surprising fact, that we haven't admitted yet, could shape our attitude toward reality in a more organic way than what we previously considered to be our starting point. In the illustration of this fact as artistic creation, it is, therefore, possible to see in Sasha Vlad's work the majestic denial of the author's style tradition: each of his automatic drawings is different from the others, which is evident in manner, as well as in genre. Some appear to be even veristic, and we can see landscapes, jungles, monsters, or nudes radiating from them, while in others it's as though they represent abstract Manchurian symbols sketched by a paintbrush onto dizzying emptiness. Here, as well, it is evident, that the resulting visions surprise the author himself, that they act as a reflection of destiny in a drop of water, or in the growth rings of a tree. I myself saw in those drawings countless events. For example, they revealed to me an exquisite varan, a three-headed beautiful woman, a horse wearing the mask of a winged lion, a streetcar in a forest, a maternity hospital for uniforms and liveries, a girl in love with an elephant, a detailed diagram of cleaning teeth, a necklace playing the role of a head, splashes into the clouds, a puppet theater in a terrarium, a terrarium in a puppet theater, a run toward a spooky cherry, an Apocalypse rider lost in a supermarket, Aquarius selling fire, hundreds of amorous combats inside a train while it is going through a tunnel, the fall of a glass of water into the water recorded by a seismogram looking like a bear falling into a barrel filled with coffee, a safety pin in the shape of a grasshopper, three Mary Magdalenes tempting God the Father, a frogman in the rib cage of a duck, a woman flute player harassed by Lohengrin, a children crusade attacking the main cemetery, the smoked tongue of a storm, an alert kestrel in front of a breathing suitcase, a wasp with a human brain in its head, rain posing by a gooseberry bush, Verne and Archimedes disguised as Dante and Virgil during their inspection of Limbo, a world-guzzler during holy communion, an epic crowd scene in dense fog, a map marking the path walked by a woman with a scythe, a portrait of a sabre-toothed ant, a clothless cancan—and so on to infinity, because every single drawing can be read in a completely different way from the way it was read the first time. Here, actually, it is as though Sasha Vlad assumes the role of nature, because it is nature that perpetually erects in front of humans images without a clue, which, actually, have the property of a *mirror*. What I saw in his drawings is undoubtedly myself. Dan Stanciu also, in his interpretation of Sasha Vlad's ciphers, has maybe experienced an Apollinairesque amazement, such as expressed by a verse from the poet's famous *Zone*: "Terrified you see yourself drawn in the agates of Saint Vitus." Sasha Vlad, admittedly, confers this mirror property to his work precisely by not aiming at consciously assigning to it any previously made up meanings: "I don't think that what I do has any expositive quality. I am not trying to explain or illustrate anything," he says.

The creative and personal coming together of both authors, who, for that matter, have been already collaborating for decades, is symptomatic for its *authenticity*. Sasha Vlad and Dan Stanciu, unlike many epigones, don't rely on style clichés, which have long since infested books, publications and webpages dedicated to putative surrealism. They strive not for surrealist style, but for surrealist thought. As emphasized by the founder of surrealism, André Breton: "...each artist must take up the search for the Golden Fleece all by oneself." From this ensues the refusal of any commonly applicable rules. On the throne of inspiration sits the *uniqueness* of creative stimuli, which depend only on the inner identity of memories, enjoyments, communications, experiences, and anticipations of every single creator, regardless of external esthetic and ideological pressures, and even regardless of any pressure of the creator's own opinions and tastes.

Thus, a creator proceeds towards discovery by taking a route, which is not traced by predecessors, but runs through trackless slopes, forgotten yards and sliding ruins. The creator then just monitors and records the naturally flowing streamlines of *Gojo particles*, which, as it is known, become luminescent when in contact with vinegar. Those streamlines,

for that matter, could be perceived by shared view, that is intersubjec-
tively, namely by the simple reason that they flow through the world
according to natural, albeit inexplicable laws on the surface—and they
apply to everyone equally. As Dan Stanciu says: "It's simple: when one
says sphere, one means bride." The *key to cognition* is the courage of
the child's vision of the world. The courage to play. This creative courage
enables one to perceive, that one and the world are, first of all, a vast
and sublime...jest.

Bruno Solarik

INDEX

31 Vibratile scaffolding surrounds, like a muff of brushwood
32 Before drying in the sun
33 On Gazelle Days, a procession of industrial ghosts
34 What makes Saint Curtain's skin different
35 When certain Tuesdays are too agitated
36 In the X zones of the Curtain
37 It's only natural that, under the rind of a sentence
38 Between the moment when a sentence dies away and the moment
39 The Antroca Intervals appear not only between sentences
40 On simple bodies
41 Miss Uno arrives the first
42 The contradictory image of Reason
43 Oftentimes, on certain less circulated seas
44 Screen-knots were
45 The lightning bolt seeds
46 Falling polyhedrons don't have arms
47 An unending row of windows
48 Between those centers go—on ropes—the gods
49 For the subgods, finding a box
50 First appears the Ascertainer
51 The first dissolving (of a black vapor in a metal)
52 In the work of a qualified Consumer
53 Non-ones are not different from non-others
54 A negative individual passing
55 A double advantage situation is that of an empty place
56 The battle between Quarters and Halves
57 The second part of the drama unfolds
58 One of the forgivable errors that a "tube" can commit
59 Now, from the muscular W placed on the M surface
60 A valley. In the valley, a river
61 In the *I Flow* dictionaries used by rivers
62 Remaking the world, by defining it, is the work
63 From the valley (every world has a valley and a hill, even the vitrified ones)
64 Nothingness or vice versa (some thing, that is)
65 The most recent *I Flow* dictionary

< Also from *Rêve à Deux* >

Will Alexander *Spectral Hieroglyphics,* 2016
Sotère Torregian *Surreal Adventurer,* 2015
Marie Wilson & Nanos Valaoritis *Land of Diamond,* 2015
Sotère Torregian *The Age of Gold (Redux),* 2012
Will Alexander *The Brimstone Boat - For Philip Lamantia,* 2012
Schlechter Duvall *The Adventures of Desirée,* 2009

Printed in the United States of America

www.ingramcontent.com/pod-product-compliance
Lightning Source LLC
Chambersburg PA
CBHW080512110426
42742CB00017B/3092